A PRISON DIARY

VOLUME ONE – BELMARSH: HELL

'Gruesome, touching, sharply written . . . the best thing Archer has written in years' – *Sunday Telegraph*

'Surprisingly effective . . . a devastating critique . . . written simply and directly' – *Sunday Times*

'The finest thing that he has ever written . . . so clear and crisp is the prose, a vivid and almost "live" account which bubbles with Dickensian detail and a Shavian sense of outrage . . . riveting' – *Independent on Sunday*

'A chilling insight into the stark reality of life in Britain's jails' – *Daily Mail*

'Truly captures the fear, the violence and the numb bleakness of prison life' – *Sunday Mirror*

'Compelling reportage . . . Jeffrey Archer raises these diaries to the standards of a prison Pepys by being such an assiduous recorder of fellow inmates' secrets'
— *nday*

JEFFREY ARCHER, whose novels and short stories include *Kane and Abel*, *A Prisoner of Birth* and *Cat O' Nine Tales*, has topped the bestseller lists around the world, with sales of over 270 million copies.

He is the only author ever to have been a number one bestseller in fiction (fifteen times), short stories (four times) and non-fiction (*The Prison Diaries*).

The author is married with two sons, and lives in London and Cambridge.

www.jeffreyarcher.com
Facebook.com/JeffreyArcherAuthor
@Jeffrey_Archer

Also by JEFFREY ARCHER

A PRISON DIARY

VOLUME ONE – BELMARSH: HELL

PAN BOOKS

First published 2002 by Macmillan

This edition published 2003 by Pan Books
an imprint of Pan Macmillan
20 New Wharf Road, London N1 9RR
Associated companies throughout the world
www.panmacmillan.com

ISBN 978-0-330-41859-1

The publishers gratefully acknowledge
Michael, Billy Little, Colin Kitto, Kenneth Chan and Derek Jones
for permission to reproduce copyright material.

37

A CIP catalogue record for this book is available from
the British Library.

Typeset by SetSystems Ltd, Saffron Walden, Essex
Printed and bound by CPI Group (UK) Ltd, Croydon, CR0 4YY

Visit **www.panmacmillan.com** to read more about all
our books and to buy them. You will also find
features, author interviews and news of any author
events, and you can sign up for e-newsletters so that
you're always first to hear about our new releases.

TO

FOUL-WEATHER FRIENDS

INVICTUS

Out of the night that covers me,
Black as the Pit from pole to pole,
I thank whatever gods may be
For my unconquerable soul.

In the fell clutch of circumstance,
I have not winced or cried aloud;
Under the bludgeonings of chance
My head is bloody, but unbowed.

Beyond this place of wrath and tears
Looms but the Horror of the shade.
And yet the menace of the years
Finds, and shall find me, unafraid.

It matters not how strait the gate,
How charged with punishments the scroll,
I am the master of my fate:
I am the captain of my soul.

William Ernest Henley (1849–1903)

BELMARSH: HELL

DAY 1   THURSDAY 19 JULY 2001

12.07 pm

'You are sentenced to four years.' Mr Justice Potts stares down from the bench, unable to hide his delight. He orders me to be taken down.

A Securicor man who was sitting beside me while the verdict was read out points towards a door on my left which has not been opened during the seven-week trial. I turn and glance at my wife Mary seated at the back of the court, head bowed, ashen-faced, a son on either side to comfort her.

I'm led downstairs to be met by a court official, and thus I begin an endless process of form-filling. Name? Archer. Age? 61. Weight? 178lbs, I tell him.

'What's that in stones?' the prison officer demands.

'12st 10lbs,' I reply. I only know because I weighed myself in the gym this morning.

'Thank you, sir,' he says, and asks me to sign on the bottom of the page.

Another Securicor man – known by the prisoners as water-rats – leads me down a long bleak cream-painted bricked corridor to I know not where.

'How long did he give you?' he asks, matter-of-factly.

'Four years,' I reply.

'Oh, not too bad, you'll be out in two,' he responds, as if discussing a fortnight on the Costa del Sol.

The officer comes to a halt, unlocks a vast steel door, and then ushers me into a cell. The room is about ten feet by five, the walls are still cream, and there is a wooden bench running along the far end. No clock, no sense of time, nothing to do except contemplate, nothing to read, except messages on the walls:

HARRY WAS HERE   FUCK ALL JUDGES
JIM DEXTER Is INOCENT, OK!

A key is turning in the lock, and the heavy door swings open. The Securicor man has returned. 'You have a visit from your legals,' he announces. I am marched back down the long corridor, barred gates are unlocked and locked every few paces. Then I am ushered into a room only slightly larger than the cell to find my silk, Nicholas Purnell QC, and his junior, Alex Cameron, awaiting me.

Nick explains that four years means two, and Mr Justice Potts chose a custodial sentence aware that I would be unable to appeal to the Parole Board for early release. Of course they will appeal on my behalf, as they feel Potts has gone way over the top. Gilly Gray QC, an old friend, had warned me the previous evening that as the jury had been out for five days and I had not entered the witness box to defend myself, an appeal might not be received too favourably. Nick adds that in any case, my appeal will not be considered before Christmas, as only short sentences are dealt with quickly.

Nick goes on to tell me that Belmarsh Prison, in Woolwich, will be my first destination.

'At least it's a modern jail,' he comments, although he warns me that his abiding memory of the place was the constant noise, so he feared I wouldn't sleep for the first few nights. After a couple of weeks, he feels confident I will be transferred to a Category D prison – an open prison – probably Ford or the Isle of Sheppey.

Nick explains that he has to leave me and return to Court No. 7 to make an application for compassionate leave, so that I can attend my mother's funeral on Saturday. She died on the day the jury retired to consider their verdict, and I am only thankful that she never heard me sentenced.

I thank Nick and Alex for all they have done, and am then escorted back to my cell. The vast iron door is slammed shut. The prison officers don't have to lock it, only unlock it, as there is no handle on the inside. I sit on the wooden bench, to be reminded that *Jim Dexter is inocent, OK!* My mind is curiously blank as I try to take in what has happened and what will happen next.

The door is unlocked again – about fifteen minutes later as far as I can judge – and I'm taken to a signing-out room to fill in yet another set of forms. A large burly officer who only grunts takes away my money clip, £120 in cash, my credit card and a fountain pen. He places them in a plastic bag. They are sealed before he asks, 'Where would you like them sent?' I give the officer Mary's name and our home address. After I've signed two more forms in triplicate, I'm handcuffed to an overweight woman of around five foot three, a cigarette dangling from the corner of her mouth. They are obviously not anticipating any trouble. She is wearing the official uniform of the prison service: a white shirt, black tie, black trousers, black shoes and black socks.

She accompanies me out of the building and on to an

3

elongated white van, not unlike a single-decker bus, except that the windows are blacked out. I am placed in what I could only describe as a cubicle – known to the recidivists as a sweatbox – and although I can see outside, the waiting press cannot see me; in any case, they have no idea which cubicle I'm in. Cameras flash pointlessly in front of each window as we wait to move off. Another long wait, before I hear a prisoner shout, 'I think Archer's in this van.' Eventually the vehicle jerks forward and moves slowly out of the Old Bailey courtyard on the first leg of a long circuitous journey to HMP Belmarsh.

As we travel slowly through the streets of the City, I spot an *Evening Standard* billboard already in place: ARCHER SENT TO JAIL. It looks as if it was printed some time before the verdict.

I am well acquainted with the journey the van is taking through London, as Mary and I follow the same route home to Cambridge on Friday evenings. Except on this occasion we suddenly turn right off the main road and into a little backstreet, to be greeted by another bevy of pressmen. But like their colleagues at the Old Bailey, all they can get is a photograph of a large white van with ten small black windows. As we draw up to the entrance gate, I see a sign declaring BELMARSH PRISON. Some wag has put a line through the B and replaced it with an H. Not the most propitious of welcomes.

We drive through two high-barred gates that are electronically operated before the van comes to a halt in a courtyard surrounded by a thirty-foot red-brick wall, with razor wire looped along the top. I once read that this is the only top-security prison in Britain from which no one has ever escaped. I look up at the wall and recall that the world record for the pole vault is 20ft 2in.

The door of the van is opened and we are let out one by one before being led off to a reception area, and then herded into a large glass cell that holds about twenty people. The authorities can't risk putting that many prisoners in the same room without being able to see exactly what we're up to. This will often be the first time co-defendants have a chance to speak to each other since they were sentenced. I sit on a bench on the far side of the wall, and am joined by a tall, well-dressed, good-looking young Pakistani, who explains that he is not a prisoner, but on remand. I ask him what he's been charged with. 'GBH – grievous bodily harm. I beat up my wife when I found her in bed with another man, and now they've banged me up in Belmarsh because the trial can't begin until she gets back from Greece, where the two of them are on holiday.'

I recall Nick Purnell's parting words, 'Don't believe anything anyone tells you in prison, and never discuss your case or your appeal.'

'Archer,' yells a voice. I leave the glass cell and return to reception where I am told to fill out another form. 'Name, age, height, weight?' the prison officer behind the counter demands.

'Archer, 61, 5ft 10, 178lbs.'

'What's that in stones?' he asks.

'12st 10lbs,' I tell him, and he fills in yet another little square box.

'Right, go next door, Archer, where you'll find my colleague waiting for you.'

This time I am met by two officers. One standing, one sitting behind a desk. The one behind the desk asks me to stand under an arc light and strip. The two officers try to carry out the entire exercise as humanely as possible. First, I take off my jacket, then my tie, followed by my shirt. 'Aquascutum, Hilditch & Key, and YSL,' says the officer who is standing up, while the other writes this information down in the appropriate box. The first officer then asks me to raise my arms above my head and turn a complete circle, while a video camera attached to the wall whirrs away in the background. My shirt is returned, but they hold on to my House of Commons cufflinks. They hand back my jacket, but not my tie. I am then asked to slip off my shoes, socks, trousers and pants. 'Church's, Aquascutum and Calvin Klein,' he announces. I complete another circle, and this time the officer asks me to lift the soles of my feet for inspection. He explains that drugs are sometimes concealed under plasters. I tell them I've never taken a drug in my life. He shows no interest. They return my pants, trousers, socks and shoes but not my leather belt.

'Is this yours?' he asks, pointing to a yellow backpack on the table beside me.

'No, I've never seen it before,' I tell him.

He checks the label. 'William Archer,' he says.

'Sorry, it must be my son's.'

The officer pulls open the zip to reveal two shirts, two pairs of pants, a sweater, a pair of casual shoes and a washbag containing everything I will need. The washbag is immediately confiscated while the rest of the clothes are placed in a line on the counter. The officer then hands me a large plastic bag with HMP Belmarsh printed in dark blue letters, supported by a crown. Everything has a logo nowadays. While I transfer the possessions I am allowed to keep into the large plastic bag, the officer tells me that the yellow backpack will be returned to my son, at the government's expense. I thank him. He looks surprised. Another officer escorts me back to the glass cell, while I cling onto my plastic bag.

This time I sit next to a different prisoner, who tells me his name is Ashmil; he's from Kosovo, and still in the middle of his trial. 'What are you charged with?' I enquire.

'The illegal importing of immigrants,' he tells me, and before I can offer any comment he adds, 'They're all political prisoners who would be in jail, or worse, if they were still in their own country.' It sounds like a well-rehearsed line. 'What are you in for?' he asks.

'Archer,' rings out the same officious voice, and I leave him to return to the reception area.

'The doctor will see you now,' the desk officer says, pointing to a green door behind him.

I don't know why I'm surprised to encounter a fresh-faced young GP, who rises from behind his desk the moment I walk in.

'David Haskins,' he announces, and adds, 'I'm sorry we have to meet in these circumstances.' I take a seat on the other side of the desk while he opens a drawer and produces yet another form.

'Do you smoke?'

'No.'

'Drink?'

'No, unless you count the occasional glass of red wine at dinner.'

'Take any drugs?'

'No.'

'Do you have any history of mental illness?'

'No.'

'Have you ever tried to abuse yourself?'

'No.'

He continues through a series of questions as if he were doing no more than filling in details for an insurance policy, to which I continue to reply, no, no, no, no and no. He ticks every box.

'Although I don't think it's necessary,' he says, looking down at the form, 'I'm going to put you in the medical wing overnight before the Governor decides which block to put you on.'

I smile, as the medical wing sounds to me like a more pleasant option. He doesn't return the smile. We shake hands, and I go back to the glass cell. I only have to wait for a few more moments before a young lady in prison uniform asks me to accompany her to the medical wing. I grab my plastic bag and follow her.

We climb three floors of green iron steps before we reach our destination. As I walk down the long corridor my heart sinks. Every person I come across seems to be in an advanced state of depression or suffering from some sort of mental illness.

'Why have they put me in here?' I demand, but she doesn't reply. I later learn that most first-time offenders spend their first night in the medical centre because it is during your first twenty-four hours in prison that you are most likely to try and commit suicide.*

I'm not, as I thought I might be, placed in a hospital ward but in another cell. When the door slams behind me I begin to understand why one might contemplate suicide. The cell measures five paces by three, and this time the brick walls are painted a depressing mauve. In one corner is a single bed with a rock-hard mattress that could well be an army reject. Against the side wall, opposite the bed, is a small square steel table and a steel chair. On the far wall next to the inch-thick iron door is a steel washbasin and an open lavatory that has no lid and no flush. I

---

* 73 people committed suicide in British prisons in 2001; 22 of them were first-time offenders. Over 1,500 prisoners attempted hanging, strangulation or suffocation in 2000, a rise of 50 per cent over the 1999 figures.

am determined not to use it.* On the wall behind the bed is a window encased with four thick iron bars, painted black, and caked in dirt. No curtains, no curtain rail. Stark, cold and unwelcoming would be a generous description of my temporary residence on the medical wing. No wonder the doctor didn't return my smile. I am left alone in this bleak abode for over an hour, by which time I'm beginning to experience a profound depression.

A key finally turns in the lock to allow another young woman to enter. She is dark-haired, short and slim, dressed in a smart striped suit. She shakes me warmly by the hand, sits on the end of the bed, and introduces herself as Ms Roberts, the Deputy Governor. She can't be a day over twenty-six.

'What am I doing here?' I ask. 'I'm not a mass murderer.'

'Most prisoners spend their first night on the medical wing,' she explains, 'and we can't make any exceptions, I'm afraid, and especially not for you.' I don't say anything – what is there to say? 'One more form to complete,' she tells me, 'that's if you still want to attend your mother's funeral on Saturday.'† I can sense that Ms Roberts is trying hard to be understanding and considerate, but I fear I am quite unable to hide my distress.

'You will be moved onto an induction block tomorrow,' she assures me, 'and just as soon as you've been categorized A, B, C, or D, we'll transfer you to another prison. I have no doubt you'll be Category D – no previous convictions, and no history of violence.' She rises from the end of the bed. Every officer carries

---

* There are no wooden items in the cell, as first-night prisoners often smash up everything.
† Nick Purnell QC asked Mr Justice Potts if I could be excused from the court to be with my mother. He refused our request. A second request was made at the beginning of the afternoon session, which he reluctantly agreed to. I reached my mother's bedside an hour before she died.

a large bunch of keys that jingle whenever they move. 'I'll see you again in the morning. Have you been able to make a phone call?' she asks as she bangs on the heavy door with the palm of her hand.

'No,' I reply as the cell door is opened by a large West Indian with an even larger smile.

'Then I'll see what I can do,' she promises before stepping out into the corridor and slamming the door closed behind her.

I sit on the end of the bed and rummage through my plastic bag to discover that my elder son, William, has included amongst my permitted items a copy of David Niven's *The Moon's a Balloon*. I flick open the cover to find a message:

> *Hope you never have to read this, Dad, but if you do, chin up,*
>   *we love you and your appeal is on its way,*
>   *William xx James xx*

Thank God for a family I adore, and who still seem to care about me. I'm not sure how I would have got through the last few weeks without them. They made so many sacrifices to be with me for every day of the seven-week trial.

There is a rap on the cell door, and a steel grille that resembles a large letter box is pulled up to reveal the grinning West Indian.

'I'm Lester,' he declares as he pushes through a pillow – rock hard; one pillow case – mauve; followed by one sheet – green; and one blanket – brown. I thank Lester and then take some considerable time making the bed. After all, there's nothing else to do.

When I've completed the task, I sit on the bed and start trying to read *The Moon's a Balloon*, but my mind continually wanders. I manage about fifty pages, often stopping to consider the jury's verdict, and although I feel tired, even exhausted, I can't begin to think about sleep. The promised phone call has not materialized, so I finally turn off the fluorescent light that shines above the bed, place my head on the rock-hard pillow and despite the agonizing cries of the patients from the cells on either side of me, I eventually fall asleep. An hour later I'm woken again when the fluorescent light is switched back on, the letter box reopens and two different eyes peer in at me – a procedure that is repeated every hour, on the hour – to make sure I haven't tried to take my own life. The suicide watch.

I eventually fall asleep again, and when I wake just after 4 am, I lie on my back in a straight line, because both my ears are aching after hours on the rock-hard pillow. I think about the verdict, and the fact that it had never crossed my mind even for a moment that the jury could find Francis innocent and me guilty of the same charge. How could we have conspired if one of us didn't realize a conspiracy was taking place? They also appeared to accept the word of my former secretary, Angie Peppiatt, a woman who stole thousands of pounds from me, while deceiving me and my family for years.

Eventually I turn my mind to the future. Determined not to waste an hour, I decide to write a daily diary of everything I experience while incarcerated.

At 6 am, I rise from my mean bed and rummage around in my plastic bag. Yes, what I need is there, and this time the authorities have not determined that it should be returned to sender. Thank God for a son who had the foresight to include, amongst other necessities, an A4 pad and six felt-tip pens.

Two hours later I have completed the first draft of everything that has happened to me since I was sent to jail.

DAY 2   FRIDAY 20 JULY 2001

8.00 am

I am woken officially – my little trapdoor is opened and I am greeted by the same warm West Indian grin, which turns to a look of surprise when he sees me sitting at the table writing. I've already been at work for nearly two hours.

'You'll be able to have a shower in a few minutes,' he announces. I've already worked out that in prison a few minutes can be anything up to an hour, so I go on writing. 'Anything you need?' he asks politely.

'Would it be possible to have some more writing paper?'

'Not something I'm often asked for,' he admits, 'but I'll see what I can do.'

Lester returns half an hour later and this time the grin has turned into a shy smile. He slips an A4 pad, not unlike the type I always use, through the little steel trap. In return he asks me for six autographs, only one to be personalized – for his daughter Michelle. Lester doesn't offer any explanation for why he needs the other five, all to be penned on separate sheets of paper. As no money can change hands in jail, we return to thirteenth-century England and rely on bartering.

I can't imagine what five Jeffrey Archer signatures are worth:

a packet of cigarettes, perhaps? But I am grateful for this trade, because I have a feeling that being allowed to write in this hellhole may turn out to be the one salvation that will keep me sane.

While I wait for Lester to return and escort me from my cell to a shower – even a walk down a long, drab corridor is something I am looking forward to – I continue writing. At last I hear a key turning and look up to see the heavy door swing open, which brings its own small sense of freedom. Lester hands me a thin green towel, a prison toothbrush and a tube of prison toothpaste before locking me back in. I clean my teeth, and my gums bleed for the first time in years. It must be some physical reaction to what I've been put through during the past twenty-four hours. I worry a little, because during my interrupted night I'd promised myself that I must remain physically and mentally fit. This, according to the prison handbook left in every cell, is nothing less than the management requires.*

After a night on the medical wing, one of my first impressions is how many of the staff, dressed in their smart, clean black uniforms, seem able to keep a smile on their face. I'm sitting on my bed wondering what to expect next, when my thoughts are interrupted by someone shouting from the other side of the block.

'Mornin', Jeff, bet you didn't expect to find yourself in 'ere.'

I look through my tiny window and across the yard to see a face staring at me from behind his own bars. Another grin. 'I'm Gordon,' he shouts. 'See you in the exercise yard in an hour or two.'

---

* They also emphasize in the same booklet that Belmarsh will not tolerate any form of bullying and they have a firm policy of no racial, ethnic or religious discrimination.

13

DAY 2

9.00 am

I'm let out of the cell and walk slowly down the corridor, to enjoy my new-found freedom, as Lester escorts me to the shower room. I feel I should let you know that in my apartment on the Albert Embankment, perhaps the facility of which I am most proud is the shower room. When I step out of it each morning, I feel a new man, ready to face the world. Belmarsh doesn't offer quite the same facilities or leave you with the same warm feeling. The large stone-floored room has three small press-button showers that issue a trickle of water which is at best lukewarm. The pressure lasts for about thirty seconds before you have to push the button again. This means a shower takes twice as long as usual but, as I am becoming aware, in prison time is the one commodity that is in abundance. Lester escorts me back to my cell, while I cling on to my small soaking towel. He tells me not to lose sight of it, because a towel has to last for seven days.

He slams the door closed.

10.00 am

I lie on my bed, staring up at the white ceiling, until my thoughts are once again interrupted by a key turning in the lock. I have no idea who it will be this time. It turns out to be a plump lady dressed in a prison uniform who has something in common with the West Indian barterer – a warm smile. She sits down on the end of my bed and hands me a form for the prison canteen. She explains that, if I can afford it, I am allowed to spend twelve pounds fifty pence a week. I must fill in the little boxes showing what I would like, and then she will see that the order is left in my cell sometime later today. I don't bother to enquire what 'sometime later' means. When she leaves, I study the canteen list meticulously, trying to identify what might be described as necessities.

I am horrified to discover that the first column on the list is dominated by several different types of tobacco, and the second column by batteries – think about it. I study the form for some considerable time, and even enjoy deciding how I will spend my twelve pounds fifty. (See pages 16–17.)

11.00 am

A bell rings, as if announcing the end of class. The cell door is opened to allow me to join the other inmates and spend forty-five minutes in the exercise yard. I'm sure you've seen this activity portrayed in many films – it's not quite the same experience when you have to participate yourself. Before going down to the yard, we all have to undergo another body search, not unlike one you might go through at an airport. We are then led down three flights of iron steps to an exercise yard at ground level.

I pace around the furlong square that is enclosed by a high red-brick wall, with a closely mown threadbare lawn in the centre. After a couple of rounds, I'm joined by Gordon, the voice who greeted me this morning from the window on the other side of the block. He turns out to be tall and slim, with the build of an athlete. He tells me without any prompting that he has already served eleven years of a fourteen-year sentence for murder. This is the fifth prison they've sent him to. Can't be for good behaviour, is my first reaction.* The author in me is curious to find out more about him, but I don't have to ask any questions because he

---

* It is not uncommon for a lifer to be moved from prison to prison, so that they can never settle or gain the upper hand.

PRISONERS NAME	NUMBER	WING AND CELL NUMBER	DATE :
ARCHER	FF 828L	MEDICAL WING	JULY 20th

TOBACCO	CODE	COST	QTY	TOTAL
GOLDEN VIRGINIA (5g)	1	£ 1.25		
Red Bull Tobacco 12.5g		£ 1.42		
UMP LIGHTER	2	£ 0.33		
	3			
MATCHES	4	£ 0.10		
B & HEDGES SINGLES	5	£ 0.22		
B & HEDGES TWENTIES	6	£ 4.35		
MARLBOROUGH TWENTIES	7	£ 4.35		
SILK CUT KINGSIZE TWENTIES	8	£ 4.35		
RONSON KINGSIZE 1x18	9	£ 3.20		
HAMLET CIGARS	10	£ 0.59		
CLAN AROMATIC	11	£ 3.39		
GOLDEN VIRGINIA 12.5g	12	£ 2.27		
OLD HOLBORN 12.5g	13	£ 2.27		
RIZALA RED / GREEN PAPERS	14	£ 0.20		
Red Bull or other brands Cig Paper	15	£ 0.12		
FILTERS	16	£ 0.52		
BATTERIES				
EVER READY R20S	19	£ 0.62		
EVER READY R14S	20	£ 0.50		
EVER READY R6S	21	£ 0.16		
ENERGISER LR20	23	£ 0.80		
ENERGISER LR14	24	£ 0.52		
ENERGISER LR6	25	£ 0.28		
EVER READY PP9	26	£ 1.90		
POSTAGE AND PHONECARDS				
1ST CLASS STAMPS (SINGLE UNIT)	241	£ 0.27		
2ND CLASS STAMPS (SINGLE UNIT)	242	£ 0.19		
STAMPS SPECIAL (SINGLE UNIT)	243	£ 0.08		
AEROGRAMMES (SINGLE UNIT)	244	£ 0.38		
PHONECARDS 1 X 20 UNITS	245	£ 2.00		
PHONECARDS 1 X 40 UNITS	246	£ 4.00		
STATIONERY / ELECTRICAL				
A4. PADS	31	1.25		
WRITING PADS	32	0.78		
ENVELOPES	33	0.75		
BIC PENS	34	0.20		
18U COLOUR PENCILS	35	1.15		
SKETCH PADS A.4	36	0.90		
HELIX RULER 30cm	37	0.40		
PLAYING CARDS	38	99p		
All Radios etc Argos Catalogue Prices Plus 6%	150			
	152			
FLASK SMALL (ENHANCED PRISONERS ONLY) 1x.05Ltr	281	6.13		
REPLACEMENT PRICE LISTS		£0.10		
	85	£0.38		
PEANUTS SALTED	86	£0.42		
	87			
KIT KAT CHUNKEY		£0.33		
MONKEY NUTS		£0.50		
TODAYS SEEDLESS RAISINS 375g /SULTANAS		£0.90		
SESAME SNAPS		£0.22		
CRESPO BLACK OLIVES POUCH		£0.65		
NESQUICK STRAWBERRY/CHOCOLATE 225g		£1.39		

CONFECTIONERY	CODE	COST	QTY	TOTAL
FUDGE Bar Cadbury's		£ 0.15		
FUSE BAR	45	£ 0.33		
CADS F / N BAR 52g	46	£ 0.35		
CADS CRUNCHIE	47	£ 0.35		
CADS CHOC ECLAIRS	48	£ 0.65		
RIPPLE	49	£ 0.33		
MALTESER	50	£ 0.35		
TOFFO ASSORTED	51	£ 0.33		
BOUNTY BAR	52	£ 0.33		
MARS 65g	53	£ 0.30		
TWIX BAR 58g	54	£ 0.42		
TUNES	55	£ 0.16		
MILKY WAY	56	£ 0.16		
SNICKERS BAR	57	£ 0.32		
MAYNARD; WINE GUMS	58	£ 0.32		
	59	£		
YORKIES	60	£ 0.35		
FRUIT PASTILLES	61	£ 0.30		
EXTRA STRONG MINTS	62	£ 0.30		
NUTS 50g / RAISINS	63	£ 0.45		
CRISPS READY SALTED	64	£ 0.28		
CRISPS CHEESE AND ONION	64	£ 0.28		
CRISPS SALT AND VINEGAR	64	£ 0.28		
CRISPS OTHER (PLEASE STATE)	64	£ 0.28		
PRINGLES READY SALTED	64	£ 0.55		
PRINGLES SOUR CREAM	64	£ 0.55		
PRINGLES SALT AND VINEGAR	64	£ 0.55		
CHEWS ASSTD		£ 0.01		
M & M PEANUTS	65	£ 0.36		
POLO MINTS	66	£ 0.21		
KIT KAT 4 FINGER		£ 0.30		
/ STARBURST		£ 0.33		
CAD FLAKE		£ 0.36		
TRACKER / LIONBAR		£ 0.32		
PICNIC		£ 0.37		
FREDO (SINGLE)		£ 0.24 15p		
BOMBAY MIX		£ 0.42		
BEVERAGES AND SOFT DRINKS				
COFFEE PLASTIC JAR	162	£ 2.35		
QUALITY TEABAGS	163	£ 0.62		
TWININGS HERBAL TEAS 1X20s		£1.17		
TWININGS HERBAL FRUITSTEAS 1X20s		£1.25	MIXED
NESCAFE COFFEE SATCHETS	199	£ 0.09		
CAPACHINO SATCHETS	196	£ 0.30		
OVALTINE	201	£ 1.57		
NESTLE CONDENSED MILK LRG	171	£ 1.65		
DRINKING CHOCOLATE 250g	177	£ 1.36		
MARVEL MILK POWDER	172	£ 1.89		
UHT WHOLE MILK/ SEMI SKIM 500m	76	£ 0.45		
UHT SOYA MILK UNSWEETENED 500ml		£0.53		
ROBINSONS APPLE / BLACK	70	£ 1.10		
ROBINSONS LEMON	71	£ 1.10		
ROBINSONS ORANGE	72	£ 1.10		
LILT CAN OR 300ml	73	£ 0.50		
COCA COLA OR DIET COKE 330ml	75	£ 0.50		
S / SPRING BOTTLES	77	£ 0.49		
T.D.Y. ORANGE JUICE	78	£ 0.68		
WATER 1.5Ltr	79	£ 0.82		
CANS 330ml FANTA	80	£ 0.50		
LUCOZADE	81	£ 2.15		
CRANBERRY JUICE		£1.16		

| PRISONER'S NAME : | | NUMBER : | | | WING & CELL NUMBER : | | DATE : | |

CARDS	CODE	COST	QTY	TOTAL	GROCERIES	CODE	COST	QTY	TOTAL
SMALL CARDS	83	£0.76			GRANULATED SUGAR 1Kg	160	£0.75		
LARGE CARDS	84	£1.16			T & L SUGAR GRAN 600g	161	£0.53		
XMAS CARDS LARGE	85				DEMERARA SUGAR 600g	164	£0.77		
XMAS CARDS SMALL	86				ROWSE HONEY 12 oz	176	£2.06		
XMAS CARDS BOX	87				ROBINSONS SQZY JAM		£1.26		
CARDS OTHER					FLORA MARGARINE	161	£0.69		
GIVE AS MUCH DETAIL AS POSSIBLE					DAIRYLEA PORTIONS	166	£0.76		
					MATURE CHEESE PORTIONS	174	£1.40		
- -					MINI CHEDDARS	138	£0.28		
					PEANUT BUTTER	138		1.62	
TOILETRIES / HEALTH PRODUCTS					POT NOODLE CHIX / MUSH	168	£0.89		
					POT NOODLE CURRY	163	£0.89		
NIVEA CREAM 25ml	104	£1.24			POT NOODLE BEEF / TOM	170	£0.89		
E45 SKIN CREAM	110	£1.95	1·95		KOKA NOODLES 85g ASSTD		£0.32		
CHAP STICK / LIPSYL	100	£1.62			GUFFA SOUP	173	£0.22		
COCOA BUTTER NATURAL LOTION 500ml	102	£0.88			HEINZ SQZY MAYONNAISE		£1.76		
COCOA BUTTER PALMERS LOTION 250ml		£3.38			HEINZ SALAD CREAM	176	£2.00		
DAX POM green 100g	103	2.07			TOMATO KETCHUP 460g	182	£1.40		
VITAMINS 60s	105	£1.77			BROWN SAUCE	184	£1.86		
COD LIVER OIL CAPSULES	106	£1.50			OXO CUBES SINGLE	185	£0.09		
DP 90 VARIOUS	107	£5.50	5·90		KELLOGS CORNFLAKES 250g	178	£1.14		
GARLIC CAPSULES	108	£1.43			KELLOGS VARIETY 12s	179	£1.59		
	110				KELLOGS RICE KRISPIES 250g	181	£1.14		
CAMAY CHIC - BLACK 100g	112	£0.45			ALPEN REGULAR	197	£1.36		
FAIRY SOAP WHITE EXTRA CARE 125g	113	£0.46			ALPEN ORIGINAL 760G		£2.60		
ZEST 125g		£0.52			WEETABIX 12s	180	£0.93		
WRIGHT COAL TAR SOAP BATH		£0.86			WEETABIX FAMILY	183	£1.57		
					KELLOGS CRUNCHY NUT C/FLAKES		£1.89		
LUX HONEY MILK SOAP	116	£0.52			QUAKER SUGAR PUFFS 320g		£1.86		
PEARS TRANSPARENT	117	£1.06			KELLOGS FRUIT & FIBRE		£1.60		
COMFORT 1 Ltr	118	£1.27			QUAKER SHREDDED WHEAT 320G		£1.16		
FLANNEL FACE	119	£0.66			KELLOGS NUTRI BARS		£0.32		
IMPERIAL LEATHER SOAP 125g	120	£0.63			READY BREAK 250g		£0.87		
JOHNSONS Babylotion 200ml	121	£2.80			JACOBS CREAM CRACKERS	186	£0.50		
JOHNSONS BABY OIL 250ml	122	£2.24			T.D.Y. RICH TEA BISCUITS	187	£0.43		
SOFTKING BABY OIL 250ml		£0.89			BOURBON CREAMS 200g	188	£0.46		
SOFTKING BABY LOTION 250ml		£0.61			RITZ CRISPS 200g	189	£0.51		
VOSENE SHAMPOO	123	£1.76			SHORTCAKE 160g	190	£0.43		
SHAMPOO TIMOTEI 250ml	124	£1.56			CUSTARD CREAMS 200g	191	£0.46		
COLGATE TOOTH PASTE 88ml	126	£0.81			NICE 160g	192	£0.43		
EUCRYL TOOTH POWDER	126	£1.42			RYVITA	193	£0.69		
STERADENT TABLETS X 30	127	£1.14			McVITIES DIGESTIVE 360g	194	£0.68		
JORDAN TOOTH BRUSH MED	128	£1.15			McVITIES HOMEWHEAT MILK	134	£0.89		
SENSODYNE TOOTH PASTE	133	£2.08			T.D.Y. GINGER NUTS 200g	200	48ª		
TOOTH PASTE ULTRA BRITE		£0.81				203	48ª		
SHAMPOO NATURAL FAMILY 500ml		£0.87			McV HOB NOBS PLAIN 300g	204	£0.96		
NATURAL FREQ CONDITIONER 500ml		£0.75			McV HOB NOBS MILK/DARK CHOC		£1.14		
SHAMPOO B/FINE PRO VIT 360ml		£1.39			COCONUT RINGS		£0.43		
SHAMPOO B/FINE 400ml		£1.39			TDY FRUIT SHORT CAKE		£0.64		
WASH N GO SHAMPOO	114	£2.30			McV JAFFA CAKES		£0.53		
SHOWER GEL NATURAL 250ml	115	£0.80			McVITIES GINGER CAKE		£0.56		
HAIR GEL 225g	136	£0.50							
DEODORANT DOVE SOLID STICK		£2.16			JOHN WEST TUNA OIL BRINE 200g		£0.30		
GILLETTE DEODORANT GEL STICK	111	£2.30			JOHN WEST CORNED BEEF 198g		£0.56		
GILLETE AFTER SHAVE BALM	137	£4.73			GLENRYCKS PILCHARDS 155g		£0.54		
TOILET ROLLS TWIN	136	£0.39			PRINCESS HAM 200g		£0.57		
TDY MANS TISSUE	445	£0.75			HOTDOGS 400g		£0.60		
PRINCES PEAR HALVES SYRUP		£0.79			HEINZ COLESLAW SALAD		£0.92		
PRINCESS PEACHES SLICED		£0.72			HEINZ POTATO SALAD		£0.81		
PINEAPPLE CRUSH IN JUICE		£0.96			VALFRUTTA SWEETCORN		£0.54		
VALFRUTTA FRUIT COCKTAIL		£0.63							
BIRDS R.T.S CUSTARD 425g		£0.95							
AMBROSIA CREAMED RICE		£0.83							

| IF THERE IS NOT ENOUGH MONEY IN YOUR ACCOUNT ORDERS WILL BE ADJUSTED FROM THE BOTTOM UPWARDS | INMATES SIGNATURE............................DATE.............. |
| CHECKED BY............................POSTED BY.................... |

never stops talking, which I later discover is a common trait among lifers.

Gordon is due out in three years' time and, although dyslexic, has taken an Open University degree in English and is now studying for a law degree. He also claims to have written a book of poetry, which I seem to recall reading something about in the *Daily Mail.*

'Don't talk to me about the press,' he screeches like a tape recorder you can't switch off. 'They always get it wrong. They said I shot my lover's boyfriend when I found them in bed together, and that he was an Old Etonian.'

'And he wasn't an Old Etonian?' I probe innocently.

'Yeah, course he was,' says Gordon. 'But I didn't shoot him, did I? I stabbed him seventeen times.'

I feel sick at this matter-of-fact revelation, delivered with neither remorse nor irony. Gordon goes on to tell me that he was twenty at the time, and had run away from home at the age of fourteen, after being sexually abused. I shuddered, despite the sun beaming down on me. I wonder just how long it will be before I'm not sickened by such confessions. How long before I don't shudder? How long before it becomes matter-of-fact, commonplace?

As we continue our circumnavigation of the yard, he points out Ronnie Biggs, who's sitting on a bench in the far corner surrounded by geraniums.

'They've just planted those, Jeff,' says Gordon. 'They must have known you were comin'.' Again, he doesn't laugh. I glance across to see a sick old man with a tube coming out of his nose. A man who doesn't look as if he has long to live.

Another circuit, before I ask Gordon about a young West Indian who has his face turned to the wall, and hasn't moved an inch since I walked into the yard.

'He killed his wife and young daughter,' says Gordon. 'He's tried to commit suicide three times since they locked him up, and doesn't talk to no one.'

I felt strangely compassionate for this double murderer as we pass him for a third time. As we overtake another man who looks totally lost, Gordon whispers, 'That's Barry George, who's just been done for killing Jill Dando.' I don't tell him that Jill was an old friend and we both hail from Weston-super-Mare. For the first time in my life, I keep my counsel. 'No one in here believes he did it,' says Gordon, 'including the screws.' I still make no comment. However, George's and my trial ran concurrently at the Old Bailey, and I was surprised by how many senior lawyers and laymen told me they were disturbed by the verdict. 'I'll bet he gets off on appeal,'* Gordon adds as another bell rings to indicate that our forty-five minutes of 'freedom' is up.

Once again we are all searched before leaving the yard, which puzzles me; if we didn't have anything on us when we came in, how could we have acquired anything while we were walking around the yard? I feel sure there is a simple explanation. I ask Gordon.

'They've got to go through the whole procedure every time,' Gordon explains as we climb back up the steps. 'It's the regulations.'

When we reach the third floor, we go our separate ways.

'Goodbye,' says Gordon, and we never meet again.

I read three days later in the *Sun* that Ronald Biggs and I shook hands after Gordon had introduced us.

---

* On 2 July 2002, Barry George lost his appeal.

DAY 2

11.45 am

Locked back up in my cell, I continue to write, only to hear the key turning before I've completed a full page. It's Ms Roberts, the Deputy Governor. I stand and offer her my little steel chair. She smiles, waves a hand, and perches herself on the end of the bed. She confirms that the arrangements for my visit to the parish church in Grantchester to attend my mother's funeral have been sanctioned by the Governor. They have checked the police computer at Scotland Yard, and as I have no previous convictions, and no history of violence, I am automatically a Category D prisoner,* which she explains is important because it means that during the funeral service the prison officers accompanying me need not wear a uniform, and therefore I will not have to be handcuffed.

The press will be disappointed, I tell her.

'It won't stop them claiming you were,' she replies.

Ms Roberts goes on to tell me that I will be moved from the medical wing to Block Three sometime after lunch. There is no point in asking her when exactly.

I resolve to spend the time that I am locked up in my cell writing, sticking to a routine I have followed for the past twenty-five years – two hours on, two hours off – though never before in such surroundings. When I normally leave home for a writing session I go in search of somewhere that has a view of the ocean.

---

* There are four categories of prisoner, A, B, C, D. A-cat are violent and dangerous prisoners, with the possible resources, i.e. money, to escape; B are violent and dangerous, but not always murderers (i.e. GBH, ABH, manslaughter or rape); C, the vast majority, are repeat offenders or convicted of a serious, non-violent crime, e.g. drug-dealers; D are usually first offence, no history of violence, often with short sentences, and likely to conform to the system, as they wish to return to society as quickly as possible.

12 noon

I'm let out of my cell to join a queue for lunch. One look at what's on offer and I can't face it – overcooked meat, Heaven knows from which animal, mushy peas swimming in water, and potatoes that Oliver Twist would have rejected. I settle for a slice of bread and a tin cup of milk, not a cup of tinned milk. I sit at a nearby table, finish lunch in three minutes, and return to my cell.

I don't have to wait long before another woman officer appears to tell me that I'm being transferred to Cell Block Three, better known by the inmates as Beirut. I pack my plastic bag which takes another three minutes while she explains that Beirut is on the other side of the prison.

'Anything must be better than the medical wing,' I venture.

'Yes, I suppose it is a little better,' she says. She hesitates. 'But not that much better.'

She escorts me along several linking corridors, unlocking and locking even more barred gates, before we arrive in Beirut. My appearance is greeted by cheers from several inmates. I learn later that bets had been placed on which block I would end up in.

Each of the four blocks serves a different purpose, so it shouldn't have been difficult to work out that I would end up on Three – the induction block. You remain in 'induction' until they have assessed you, like a plane circling above an airport waiting to be told which runway you can finally land on. More of that later.

My new cell turns out to be slightly larger, by inches, and a little more humane, but, as the officer promised, only just. The walls are an easier-to-live-with shade of green, and this time the lavatory has a flush. No need to pee in the washbasin any more.

The view remains consistent. You just stare at another red-brick block, which also shields all human life from the sun. The long walk from the medical block across the prison to Block Three had itself served as a pleasant interlude, but I feel sick at the thought of this becoming a way of life.

A tea-boy or Listener* called James is waiting outside my cell to greet me. He has a kind face, and reminds me of a prefect welcoming a new boy on his first day at school, the only difference being that he's twenty years younger than I am. James tells me that if I need any questions answered I should not hesitate to ask. He advises me not to say anything to anyone – prisoners or officers – about my sentence or appeal, or to discuss any subject I don't want to see in a national newspaper the following day. He warns me that the other prisoners all believe they're going to make a fortune by phoning the *Sun* to let a journalist know what I had for lunch. I thank him for the advice my QC has already proffered. James passes over another rock-hard pillow with a green pillowcase, but this time I'm given two sheets and two blankets. He also hands me a plastic plate, a plastic bowl, a plastic mug and a plastic knife and fork. He then tells me the bad news, England were all out for 187. I frown.

'But Australia are 27 for two,' he adds with a grin. He's obviously heard about my love of cricket. 'Would you like a radio?' he asks. 'Then you can follow the ball-by-ball commentary.'

I cannot hide my delight at the thought, and he leaves me while I make up my new bed. He returns a few minutes later with a battered black radio, from I know not where.

---

* Selected prisoners are invited to become Listeners. They are then trained by the Samaritans so that they can assist fellow inmates who are finding prison hard to come to terms with, especially those contemplating suicide.

'I'll see you later,' he says and disappears again.

I take a considerable time balancing the radio on the tiny brick window sill with the aerial poking out between the bars before I am able to tune into the familiar voice of Christopher Martin-Jenkins on *Test Match Special*. He's telling Blowers that he needs a haircut. This is followed by the more serious news that Australia are now 92 for 2, and both the Waugh brothers look set in their ways. As it's an off-writing period, I lie down on the bed and listen to Graham Gooch's groan as two catches are dropped in quick succession. By the time a bell goes for supper, Australia are 207 for 4, and I suspect are on the way to another innings victory.

6.00 pm

Once again I reject the prison food, and wonder how long it will be before I have to give in.

I return to my cell to find my purchases from the canteen list have been left on the end of my bed. Someone has entered my cell and left without my knowing, is strangely my first reaction. I pour a cup of Buxton water into my plastic mug, and remove the lid from a tube of Pringles. I eat and drink very slowly.

7.00 pm

Three hours later another bell rings. All the cell doors are opened by prison officers and the inmates congregate on the ground floor for what is known as 'Association'. This is the period when you mix with the other prisoners for one hour. As I walk the longest route I can circumnavigate – walking is now a luxury – I discover what activities are on offer. Four black men wearing gold chains with crosses attached are sitting in one corner playing dominoes. I discover later that all four of them are in for murder. None of them appears particularly violent as they consider their next move. I walk on to see two more inmates playing pool, while others lounge around reading the *Sun* – by far the most popular paper in the prison if one is to judge on a simple head count. At the far end of the room is a long queue for the two phones. Each waiting caller has a £2 phonecard which they can use at any time during Association. I'm told I will receive one tomorrow. Everything is tomorrow. I wonder if in a Spanish jail everything is the day after tomorrow?

I stop and chat to someone who introduces himself as Paul. He tells me that he's in for VAT fraud (seven years), and is explaining how he got caught when we are joined by a prison officer. A long conversation follows during which the officer reveals that he also doesn't believe Barry George killed Jill Dando.

'Why not?' I ask.

'He's just too stupid,' the officer replies. 'And in any case, Dando was killed with one shot, which convinces me that the murder must have been carried out by a disciplined professional.' He goes on to tell us that he has been on the same spur as George for the past eighteen months and repeats, 'I can tell you he's just not up to it.'

Pat (murder, reduced to manslaughter, four years) joins us, and says he agrees. Pat recalls an incident that took place on 'prison sports day' last year, when Barry George – then on remand – was running in the one hundred yards and fell over at thirty. 'He's a bit of a pervert,' Pat adds, 'and perhaps he ought to be locked up, but he's no murderer.'

When I leave them to continue my walkabout, I observe that we are penned in at both ends of the room by a floor-to-ceiling steel-mesh sheet. Everyone nods and smiles as I pass, and some prisoners stop me and want to talk about their upcoming trials, while others who are sending out cards need to know how to spell Christine or Suzanne. Most of them are friendly and address me as Lord Jeff, yet another first. I try to look cheerful. When I remember that if my appeal fails the minimum time I will have to serve is two years, I can't imagine how anyone with a life sentence can possibly cope.

'It's just a way of life,' says Jack, a forty-eight-year-old who has spent the last twenty-two years in and out of different prisons. 'My problem,' he adds, 'is I'm no longer qualified to do anything when I get out.'

The last person who told me that was a Conservative Member of Parliament a few days before the last election. He lost.

Jack invites me to visit his cell on the ground floor. I'm surprised to find three beds in a room not much larger than mine. I thought he was about to comment on how lucky I was to have a single cell, but no, he simply indicates a large drawing attached to the wall.

'What do you think that is, Jeff?' he demands.

'No idea,' I reply. 'Does it tell you how many days, months or years you still have to go before you're released?'

'No,' Jack responds. He then points below the washbasin where a small army of ants are congregating. I'm a bit slow and still haven't put two and two together. 'Each night,' Jack goes on to explain, 'the three of us organize ant races, and that's the track. A sort of ants' Ascot,' he adds with a laugh.

'But what's the stake?' I enquire, aware that no one is allowed to have any money inside a prison.

'On Saturday night, the one who's won the most races during the week gets to choose which bed they'll sleep in for the next seven days.'

I stare at the three beds. On one side of the room, up against the wall, is a single bed while on the other side are bunk beds.

'Which does the winner choose?'

'You're fuckin'* dumb, Jeff. The top one, of course; that way you're farthest away from the ants, and can be sure of a night's sleep.'

'What do the ants get?' I ask.

'If they win, they stay alive until the next race.'

'And if they lose?'

'We put them into tomorrow's soup.' I think it was a joke.

Another bell sounds and the officers immediately corral us back into our cells and slam the doors shut. They will not be unlocked again until eight tomorrow morning.

A senior officer stops me as I am returning to my cell to tell me that the Governor wants a word. I follow him, but have to halt every few yards as he unlocks and locks countless iron-barred gates before I'm shown into a comfortable room with a sofa, two easy chairs and pictures on the wall.

Mr Peel, the Governor of Block Three, rises and shakes my hand before motioning me to an easy chair. He asks me how I am settling in. I assure him that the medical wing isn't something I'd want to experience ever again. Block Three, I admit, although dreadful, is a slight improvement.

Mr Peel nods, as if he's heard it all before. He then explains that there are five Governors at Belmarsh, and he's the one responsible for arranging my visit to Grantchester to attend my mother's funeral. He goes on to confirm that everything is in place, but I must be ready to leave at seven o'clock tomorrow morning. I'm about to ask why seven o'clock when the service

---

*I will only use foul language when it's reported in speech, which for most inmates is every sentence. Fuckin' is the only adjective they ever bother with.

isn't until eleven, and the journey to Grantchester usually takes about an hour, when he rises from his place and adds, 'I'll see you again just as soon as you've returned from Cambridge.'

Mr Peel says goodnight but doesn't shake hands a second time. I leave his office and try to find the way back to my cell. As I'm unescorted, I lose my way. An officer quickly comes to my rescue and guides me back on the straight and narrow, obviously confident that I wasn't trying to escape. I couldn't find my way in, let alone out, I want to tell him.

9.00 pm

Once locked back up in my tiny room, I return to *The Moon's a Balloon* and read about David Niven's first experience of sex, and laugh, yes laugh, for the first time in days. At eleven, I turn off my light. Two West Indians on the same floor are shouting through their cell windows, but I can neither follow nor understand what they are saying.* They go on hollering at each other like a married couple who ought to get divorced.

I have no idea what time it was when I fell asleep.

---

* This is a common experience in most jails, and can go on all night. They are known as 'window warriors'.

DAY 3   SATURDAY 21 JULY 2001

4.07 am

I wake a few minutes after four, but as I am not due to be picked up until seven I decide to write for a couple of hours. I find I'm writing more slowly now that there are so few distractions in my life.

6.00 am

An officer unlocks my cell door and introduces himself as George. He asks me if I would like to have a shower. My towel has been hanging over the end of my bed all night and is still damp, but at least they've supplied me with a Bic razor so that I can set about getting rid of two days' growth. I consider cutting my throat, but the thought of failure and the idea of having to return to the hospital wing is enough to put anyone off. The experience of that medical wing must deter most prisoners from harming themselves, because it's not the easy option. If you are sent back to the top floor you'd better be ill, or you will be by the time they've finished with you.

I go off to have my shower. I'm getting quite good at anticipating when to press the button so that the flow of water doesn't stop.

7.00 am

'Are you ready?' George asks politely.

'Yes,' I say, 'except that my black tie has been confiscated along with my cufflinks.'

George's fellow officer hands me a black tie, and a pair of cufflinks materialize. I can only assume that they had anticipated my problem. I point out to George that his black tie is smarter than mine.

'Possibly, but mine's a clip-on,' he says, 'otherwise I'd happily lend it to you.'

'A clip-on?' I repeat in mock disdain.

'Prison regulations,' he explains. 'No officer ever wears a tie as it puts him at risk of being strangled.'

I learn something new every few minutes.

The two of them escort me to the front hall, but not before we've passed through seven double-bolted floor-to-ceiling barred gates. When we reach the reception area, I am once again strip-searched. The officers carry out this exercise as humanely as possible, though it's still humiliating.

I am then taken out into the yard to find a white Transit van awaiting me. Once inside, I'm asked to sit in the seat farthest from the door. George sits next to the door, while his colleague slips into the spare seat directly behind him. The tiny windows are covered with bars and blacked out; I can see out, though no one can see in. I tell George that the press are going to be very frustrated.

'There were a lot of them hanging round earlier this morning waiting for you,' he tells me, 'but a high-security van left about an hour ago at full speed and they all chased after it. They'll be halfway to Nottingham before they realize you're not inside.'

The electric gates slide open once again, this time to let me out. I know the journey to Cambridge like the clichéd 'back of my hand' because I've made it once, sometimes twice, a week for the past twenty years. But this time I am taken on a route that I never knew existed, and presume it can only be for security reasons. I once remember John Major's driver telling me that he knew twenty-two different routes from Chequers to No. 10, and another twenty back to Huntingdon, and none of them was the most direct.

I find it a little stifling in the back of the van. There is no contact with the driver in the front, or the policeman sitting beside him, because they are sealed off, almost as if they're in a separate vehicle. I sense that George and his colleague are a little nervous – I can't imagine why, because I have no intention of trying to escape, as I abhor any form of violence. I learn later they are nervous because should anything go wrong they'll be blamed for it – and something does go wrong.

When we reach the M11, the van remains at a steady fifty on the inside lane, and I begin to feel sick cooped up in that armour-plated compartment on wheels. Our first destination is the Cambridge Crematorium, which is situated on the north side of the city, so when we come off the motorway at exit thirteen, I'm surprised to find that the driver turns left, and starts going in the wrong direction. We travel for a couple of miles towards Royston, before pulling into a large car park attached to the Siemens Building.

George explains that Siemens is where they have agreed to liaise with the local police before travelling on to the crematorium. One enterprising black-leather-clad motorcyclist (journalist) who spotted the van coming off the roundabout at exit thirteen has followed us to the Siemens Building. He skids to a halt, and immediately taps out some numbers on his mobile phone. The policeman seated in the front makes it clear that he wants to be on the move before any of the biker's colleagues join him. But as we have to wait for the local police before we can proceed, we're stuck.

It is of course unusual to have a cremation before the church service, but the crematorium was free at 10 am and the church not until midday. The following day the press come up with a dozen reasons as to why the funeral had been conducted in this order – from the police demanding it, through to me wanting to fool them. Not one of them published the correct reason.

Within minutes, the police escort arrives and we are on our way.

When we drive into the crematorium, there are over a hundred journalists and photographers waiting for us behind a barrier that has been erected by the police. They must have been disappointed to see the white van disappear behind the back of the building, where they slipped me in through the entrance usually reserved for the clergy.

Peter Walker, an old friend and the former Bishop of Ely, is waiting to greet us. He guides me through to a little room, where he will put on his robes and I will change into a new suit, which my son William is bringing over from the Old Vicarage. I will be only too happy to be rid of the clothes I've been wearing for the past few days. The smell of prison is a perfume that even Nicole Kidman couldn't make fashionable.

The Bishop takes me through the cremation service, which, he says, will only last for about fifteen minutes. He confirms that the main funeral service will be conducted in the Parish Church of St Andrew and St Mary in Grantchester at twelve o'clock.

A few minutes later, my immediate family arrive via the front door and have to face the clicking cameras and the shouted questions. Mary is wearing an elegant black dress with a simple brooch that my mother left her in her will. She is ashen-faced, which was my last memory of her before I left the dock. I begin to accept that this terrible ordeal may be even more taxing for my family who are trying so hard to carry on their daily lives while not letting the world know how they really feel.

When Mary comes through to join me in the back, I hold on to her for some time. I then change into my new suit, and go through to the chapel and join the rest of the family. I greet each one of them before taking my place in the front row, seated between William and Mary. I try hard to concentrate on the fact that we are all gathered together in memory of my mother, Lola, but it's hard to forget I'm a convict, who in a few hours' time will be back in prison.

10.30 am

The Bishop conducts the service with calm and quiet dignity, and when the curtains are finally drawn around my mother's coffin, Mary and I walk forward and place a posy of heather next to the wreath.

Mary leaves by the front door, while I return to the back room where I am greeted by another old friend. The two prison officers are surprised when Inspector Howell from the local constabulary says, 'Hello, Jeffrey, sorry to see you in these circumstances.'

I explain to them that when I was Chairman of Cambridge Rugby Club, David was the 1st XV skipper, and the best scrum-half in the county.

'How do you want to play it?' I ask.

David checks his watch. 'The service at Grantchester isn't for another hour, so I suggest we park up at Cantalupe Farm, and wait at the Old Vicarage, until it's time to leave for the church.'

I glance at George to see if this meets with his approval. 'I'm happy to fall in with whatever the local constabulary advise,' he says.

I'm then driven away to Cantalupe Farm in my armoured van, where the owner, Antony Pemberton, has kindly allowed us to park. Mary and the boys travel separately in the family car. We then all make our way by foot over to the Old Vicarage accompanied by only a couple of photographers as the rest of the press are massed outside St Andrew's; they have all assumed that we would be travelling directly to the parish church.

We all wait around in the kitchen for a few moments, while Mary Anne, our housekeeper, makes some tea, pours a large glass of milk and cuts me a slice of chocolate cake. I then ask George if I might be allowed to walk around the garden.

The Old Vicarage at Grantchester (circa 1680) was, at the beginning of the last century, the home of Rupert Brooke. The beautiful garden has been tended for the past fifteen years by my wife and Rachael, the gardener. Between them they've turned it from a jungle into a haven. The trees and flowerbeds are exquisite and the walks to and from the river quite magnificent. George and his colleague, though never more than a few paces away, remain out of earshot, so Mary and I are able to discuss my appeal. She reveals an amazing piece of new evidence concerning Mr Justice Potts that, if substantiated, could cause there to be a retrial.

Mary then goes over the mistakes she thinks the judge made during the trial. She is convinced that the appeal judges will at least reduce my four-year sentence.

'You don't seem pleased,' she adds as we walk along the bank of the River Cam.

'For the first time in my life,' I tell her, 'I assume the worst, so that if anything good happens, I'll be pleasantly surprised.' I've become a pessimist overnight.

33

We return from the river bank, walk back towards the house and over a wooden bridge that spans Lake Oscar – in reality it's a large pond full of koi carp, named after one of my wife's favourite cats, who after five years of purring and pawing at the water's edge failed to catch a single fish. After feeding our Japanese and Israeli immigrants, we return to the house and prepare ourselves to face the press.

David Howell says that he doesn't want me driven to the church in a police car and suggests that I accompany Mary and the family on foot for the four-hundred-yard walk from the Old Vicarage to the parish church. The police and the prison officers are doing everything in their power to remember that the occasion is my mother's funeral.

11.35 am

We leave by the front door, to find a crowd of journalists, photographers and cameramen waiting outside the gates. I estimate their number to be about a hundred (George later tells the Governor over his mobile phone that it's nearer two hundred). My younger son, James, and his girlfriend Talita, lead the little party on the quarter-mile journey to the church. They are followed by William and my adopted sister, Liz, with Mary and myself bringing up the rear. The cameramen literally fall over each other as they try to get their shots while we make our way slowly up to the parish church. One ill-mannered lout shouts questions at us, so I turn and talk to Mary. He only gives up when he realizes none of us is going to grace him with a reply. I find myself feeling bitter for the first time in my life.

When we reach the church door I am greeted by my cousin Peter, who is handing out copies of the Order of Service, while his wife Pat guides us to a pew in the front row. I'm touched by how many of my mother's friends have travelled from all over the world to attend the little service – from America, Canada and even Australia – not to mention many friends from the West Country where she spent most of her life.

The Order of Service has been selected by Mary and reveals so much about the thought and preparation my wife puts into everything. She must have taken hours selecting the prayers, hymns, readings and music, and she hits just the right note. Bishop Walker once again officiates, and my stepbrother, David Watson, gives a moving address in which he recalls my mother's boundless energy, love of learning and wicked sense of humour.

I read the final lesson, Revelation XXI, verses 1–7, and as I face the congregation, wonder if I'll manage to get the words out. I'm relieved to discover that I don't have to spend those final moments with my mother accompanied by the press, as they at least have had the courtesy to remain outside.

The service lasts for fifty minutes, and is about the only time that day when I can concentrate on my mother and her memory. Not for the first time am I thankful that she didn't live to see me convicted, and my thoughts turn to the sacrifices she made to ensure I had a decent education, and was given as good a start as possible, remembering that my father died leaving debts of around five hundred pounds, and mother had to go out to work to make ends meet. I tried in the later years to make life a little easier for her, but I was never able to repay her properly.

The service ends with 'Jesu, Joy of Man's Desiring', and Mary and I follow the Bishop and the choir down the aisle. When we reach the vestry, George immediately joins us. A member of the press has called Belmarsh to ask why I was allowed to return to the Old Vicarage.

'You'll have to say your goodbyes here, I'm afraid,' he tells us. 'The Governor has phoned to say you can't go back to the house.' I spend the next few minutes shaking hands with every-one who has attended the service and am particularly touched by the presence of Donald and Diana Sinden, who my mother adored.

After thanking the Bishop, my family join me as we begin the long slow walk back to the prison van parked at Cantalupe Farm. I glance to my left as we pass the Old Vicarage. This time the press become even more frantic. They begin to holler out their questions like a repeater gun.

'Are you expecting to remain a lord?'

'Do you hope to win your appeal?'

'Do you want to say anything about your mother?'

'Do you consider yourself a criminal?'

After about a hundred yards or so they finally give up, so Mary and I chat about her forthcoming trip to Strathclyde University, where she will chair a summer school on solar energy. The date has been in her diary for some months, but she offers to cancel the trip and stay in London so she can visit me in Belmarsh. I won't hear of it, as I need her to carry on as normal a life as possible. She sighs. The truth is, I never want Mary to see me in Belmarsh.

When we reach the van, I turn back to look at the Old Vicarage, which I fear I won't be seeing again for some time. I then hug my family one by one, leaving Mary to last. I look across to see my driver David Crann in tears – the first time in fifteen years I've seen this former SAS warrior show any vul-nerability.

On the slow journey back to Belmarsh, I once again consider what the future holds for me, and remain convinced I must above all things keep my mind alert and my body fit. The writing of a day-to-day diary seems to be my best chance for the former, and a quick return to the gym the only hope for the latter.

3.07 pm

Within moments of arriving back at Belmarsh, I'm put through another strip-search before being escorted to my cell on Block Three. Once again, James the Listener is waiting for me. He has from somewhere, somehow, purloined a carton of milk, a new razor* and two, yes two, towels. He perches himself on the end of the bed and tells me there is a rumour that they are going to move me to another block on Monday, as Beirut is only the induction wing.

'What's the difference?' I ask.

'If you're going to be here for a couple of weeks, they have to decide which block to put you on while you're waiting to be transferred to a D-cat. I think you're going to Block One,' says James, 'so you'll be with the lifers.'

'Lifers?' I gasp. 'But doesn't that mean I'll be locked up all day and night?'

'No, no,' says James. 'The lifers have a much more relaxed regime than any other block, because they keep their heads down and don't want to be a nuisance. It's the young ones who are on remand or doing short sentences that cause most of the trouble and therefore have to be locked up first.'

It's fascinating to discover how much of prison life is the exact opposite to what you would expect.

James then gives me the bad news. He's going to be transferred to Whitemoor Prison tomorrow morning, so I won't be seeing him again, but he has already allocated another inmate called Kevin to be my Listener.

'Kevin's a good guy,' he assures me, 'even if he talks too much. So if he goes on a bit, just tell him to shut up.'

---

* You're allowed one Bic razor a day, and not until you hand in your old one will they supply you with a new one. It was several days before I discovered why.

Before James leaves, I can't resist asking him what he's in for.

'Smuggling drugs from Holland,' he replies matter-of-factly.

'And you were caught?'

'Red-handed.'

'How much were the drugs worth?'

'The police claimed a street value of £3.3 million. I can only imagine it must have been Harley Street,' adds James with a wry smile.

'How much did you receive for doing the job?'

'Five thousand pounds.'

'And your sentence?'

'Six years.'

'And Kevin?' I ask. 'What's he in for?'

'Oh, he was on that Dome jewellery caper, driving one of the getaway boats – trouble was he didn't get away.' James pauses. 'By the way,' he says, 'the staff tell me that you aren't eating.'

'Well, that's not quite accurate,' I reply. 'But I am living on a diet of bottled water, KitKat and Smith's crisps, but as I'm only allowed to spend twelve pounds fifty a week, I'm already running out of my meagre provisions.'

'Don't worry,' he says. 'You'll be allowed another canteen list once they've transferred you to a new wing, so fill yours in tonight and Kevin can hand it in first thing in the morning.'

I smile at the man's ingenuity and see why the prison officers have made him a Listener. They obviously, like LBJ,* feel it's better to have him pissing out of the tent, rather than pissing in.

James then changes the subject to the leadership of the Conservative Party. He wants Kenneth Clarke to be the next leader, and he's disappointed that Michael Portillo missed the cut by one vote, because he's never heard of Iain Duncan Smith.

---

* Lyndon Baines Johnson, the thirty-sixth President of the United States.

'Why Clarke?' I ask.

'His brother was the Governor of Holloway, and has the reputation of being a fair and decent man. Mr Clarke strikes me as the same sort of bloke.' I have to agree with James, feeling that he's summed up Ken rather well.

4.30 pm

James leaves when Mr Weedon appears by the door, impatient to lock me back in. I'm beginning to learn the names of the officers. I check my watch, it's just after four thirty. Mr Weedon explains that as it's a Saturday and they're short-staffed, they won't be opening the door again until nine o'clock the next morning. As the cell door slams shut, I reflect on the fact that for the next seventeen hours I will be left alone in a room nine feet by six.

6.00 pm

I feel very low. This is the worst period of the day. You think of your family and what you might be doing at this time on a Saturday evening – James and I would have been watching the Open Golf from Lytham & St Anne's, hoping against hope that Colin Montgomerie would at last win a major. William might be reading a book by some obscure author I'd never heard of. Mary would probably be in the folly at the bottom of the garden working on volume two of her book, *Molecular to Global Photosynthesis*, and around seven I would drive across to Saffron Walden to visit my mother, and discuss with her who should lead the Tory Party.

My mother is dead. James is in London with his girlfriend.

DAY 3

William is on his way back to New York. Mary is at the Old Vicarage alone, and I'm locked up in jail.

10.00 pm

It's dark outside – no curtains to cover my little cell window. I'm exhausted. I pick up one of my new towels, fold it, and place it across my pillow. I lower my head onto the towel and sleep, disturbed only by what I assume is a fire-alarm test at 3 am.

DAY 4   SUNDAY 22 JULY 2001

5.43 am

I wake to find my tiny cell filled with sunlight. I place my feet on the floor and can smell my own body. I decide that the first thing I must do is have a long shave before even thinking about a writing session. As soon as they unlock the door, I'll make a dash for the showers.

There's no plug in the basin so I decide to improvise, and fill my plastic soup bowl with warm water and turn it into a shaving bowl.* The prison have supplied a stick of shaving soap, an old-fashioned shaving brush – I don't think it's badger hair – and a plastic Bic razor, not unlike the one you're given when travelling on British Airways (economy). It takes me some time to build up any lather. Above the basin is a steel-plated mirror measuring four inches square which reflects a blurred image of a tired, bristly man. After my shave in lukewarm water, I feel a lot better, even though I've cut myself several times.

I return to my chair behind the little square table, and with my back to the window begin writing. The sun is shining through the four panes of glass, reproducing a shadow of the

---

* I discovered later that you can buy a plug from the canteen for 25p, but if you leave your cell door open for more than a minute, it disappears.

DAY 4

bars on the wall in front of me – just in case I should forget where I am.

9.01 am

The key turns in the lock and my cell door is pushed open. I look up at an officer who has a puzzled expression on his face.

'What's happened to your cell card?' he asks. He's referring to a white card* attached to my cell door stating my name – Archer, D-cat, release date July 19th, 2005.

'It's been removed,' I explain. 'I've had six of them in the past two days. I think you'll find they've become something of a collector's item.'

Despite the absence of my card, the officer allows me to go off to the shower room, where I join a group of noisy prisoners who are looking forward to an afternoon visit from their families. One of them, a black guy called Pat, carries a clean, freshly-ironed white shirt on a hanger. I'm full of admiration and ask how he managed it, explaining that my children are coming to see me in a couple of days and I'd like to look my best.

'I'll send round my man to see you, your Lordship,' Pat says with a grin. 'He'll take care of you.'

I thank Pat, not quite sure if he's teasing me. Once I've completed another press-button shower – I've almost mastered it – and dried myself, I return to my cell to have breakfast. Breakfast was handed to me last night in a plastic bag, only moments after I'd rejected the evening meal. I extract a very hard-boiled egg from the bag, before disposing of the rest of its

---

* White cards denote Church of England, red cards Roman Catholic, yellow, Muslim, and green, Jewish. This is to show any dietary needs, and if you are attending a service when you should be locked up.

contents in the plastic bucket under the sink. While eating the egg – white only, avoiding the yolk – I stare out of my window and watch the planes as they descend at regular, sixty-second intervals into City Airport. A pigeon joins me on the ledge, but he's on the outside. I retrieve a piece of stale bread from the bucket under the washbasin, break it into small crumbs and drop them on the sill. He rejects my offering, coos and flies away.

9.30 am

The cell is unlocked again, this time for Association, and the duty officer asks me if I want to attend a church service. Not being utterly convinced there is a God I rarely go to church in Grantchester, despite the fact that my wife was for many years the choir-mistress. However, on this occasion it will mean a long walk and forty-five minutes in a far larger room than my cell, so without hesitation I thank God and say yes.

'RC or Church of England?' the officer enquires.

'C of E,' I reply.

'Then you'll be on the second shift. I'll call you around 10.30 straight after Association.'

10.00 am

During Association, prison officers watch to see if you become part of a clique or gang, and how you behave while in a group, or if you're simply a loner. I'm about to leave my cell, only to find a queue of prisoners waiting at my door. Most of them want autographs so they can prove to their partners or girlfriends that they were on the same block as the notorious Jeffrey Archer.

When I've finished what can only be described as a signing session not unlike the ones I usually carry out at Hatchard's, I'm joined by my new Listener, Kevin. He confirms that James was shipped out to Whitemoor early this morning.

'So what do you need, Jeffrey? Can I call you Jeffrey?'

'Of course. What do I need?' I repeat. 'How about a bowl of cornflakes with some real milk, two eggs, sunny side up, bacon, mushrooms and a cup of hot chocolate.'

Kevin laughs. 'I can sort out some Weetabix, skimmed milk, fresh bread. Anything else?'

'A decent razor, some shampoo, a bar of soap and a change of towels?'

'That may take a little longer,' he admits.

As everyone knows what I'm in for, I ask the inevitable question.

'I was part of the Dome jewellery raid, wasn't I,' he says as if everybody was.

What a sentence to deliver to an author. 'How did you become involved?' I ask.

'Debt,' he explains, 'and a measure of bad luck.'

Nick Purnell's words rang in my ears. *Don't believe anything you're told in prison, and never reveal to your fellow inmates any details of your own case.* 'Debt?' I repeat.

'Yeah, I owed a man thirteen hundred pounds, and although I hadn't spoken to him for over a year, he suddenly calls up out of the blue and demands to see me.' I don't interrupt the flow. 'We met up at a pub in Brighton where he told me he needed a speedboat and driver for a couple of hours and if I was willing to do it, I could forget the debt.'

'When did he expect you to carry out the job?' I ask.

'The next morning,' Kevin replied. 'I told him I couldn't consider it because I'd already got another job lined up.'

'What job?' I asked.

'Well, my dad and I've got a couple of boats that we fish off

44

the coast, and they were both booked for the rest of the week. "Then I want my money," the man demanded, so I wasn't left with a lot of choice. You see, I was skint at the time, and anyway, he had a reputation as a bit of a hard man, and all he wanted me to do was transport four men from one side of the river to the other. The whole exercise wouldn't take more than ten minutes.'

'One thousand three hundred pounds for ten minutes' work? You must have realized that there was a catch?'

'I was suspicious, but had no idea what they were really up to.'

'So what happened next?'

'I took the boat as instructed up to Bow Creek, moored it near the jetty a few hundred yards from the Dome and waited. Suddenly all hell broke loose. Three police boats converged on me, and within minutes I was surrounded by a dozen armed officers shouting at me to lie down on the deck with my hands above my head. One of them said, "Blimey it's not him," and I later discovered that I'd been brought in at the last minute to replace someone who had let the gang down.'

'But by then you must have known what they were up to?'

'Nope,' he replied, 'I'm thirty-five years old, and this is my first offence. I'm not a criminal, and after what my family and I have been put through, I can tell you I won't be coming back to prison again.'

I can't explain why I wanted to believe him. It might have been his courteous manner, or the way he talked about his wife and fourteen-year-old son. And he was certainly going to pay dearly for a foolish mistake; one that he would regret for the rest of his life.*

---

* Kevin Meredith was tried and convicted at the Old Bailey on 18 February 2002 for conspiracy to steal, and sentenced to five years' imprisonment.

DAY 4

'Archer, Collins, Davies, Edwards,' booms the voice of Mr King, an officer not given to subtlety as he continues to bellow out names until he comes to Watts, before adding, 'C of E, now.'

'I think we'll have to continue this conversation at some other time,' I suggest. 'Our Lord calls and if he doesn't, Mr King certainly does.' I then join the other prisoners who are waiting on the middle landing to be escorted to the morning service.

11.00 am

A crocodile of prisoners proceeds slowly along the polished linoleum floor until we're stopped for another body search before entering the chapel. Why would they search us before going into a place of worship? We file into a large hall where each worshipper is handed a Bible. I take my place in the second row next to a young black man who has his head bowed. I glance around at what appears to be a full house.

The Chaplain, David (his name is written in bold letters on a label attached to his well-worn jacket), takes his place at the front of the chapel and calls for silence. He is a man of about forty-five, stockily built, with a pronounced limp and a stern smile. He stares down at his congregation of murderers, rapists, burglars and wife-beaters. Not surprisingly, it takes him a couple of minutes to bring such a flock to order.

While he goes about his task, I continue to look around the room. It's square in shape, and I would guess measures about twenty paces by twenty. The outer walls are red brick and the room holds about two hundred plastic chairs, in rows of twenty. On the four walls there are paintings of Christ and his Disciples, Christ being carried to the tomb after being taken down from the Cross, the Virgin Mother with an angel, the Raising of Lazarus, and Christ calming the storm.

Directly behind the Chaplain is a rock band – their leader is a pretty, dark-haired girl who has a guitar slung over her shoulder. She is accompanied by five Gospel singers, all of whom have tiny microphones pinned to their lapels. In front of the group is a man seated with his back to the congregation. He is working a slide projector that flashes up on a white sheet hung in front of him the words of the first hymn.

When the Chaplain finally gains silence – achieved only after a threat that anyone caught talking would immediately be escorted back to their cell – he begins the service by delivering three prayers, all unsubtly spelling out the simple message of doing good by your neighbour. He then turns to the girl with the guitar and gives her a slight bow. Her gentle voice rings out the melody of the first hymn, more of a Gospel message, which is accompanied heartily by the black prisoners who make up well over half the congregation, while the rest of us are a little more reserved. The group's backing singers are all white, and give as good as they get, even when the clapping begins. After the last verse has rung out, we are all ready for the sermon, and what a sermon it turns out to be.

The Chaplain's chosen theme is murder. He then invites us to pick up our Bibles – which he describes as the biggest bestseller of all time – and turn to the book of Genesis. He glances in my direction and winks.

'And it all began with Cain and Abel,' he tells us, 'because Cain was the first murderer. Envious of his brother's success, he gained revenge by killing him. But God saw him do it and punished him for the rest of his life.'

His next chosen example of a murderer was Moses, who, he told us, killed an Egyptian and also thought he'd got away with it, but he hadn't because God had seen him, so he too was punished for the rest of his life. I don't remember that

47

bit, because I thought Moses died peacefully in his bed aged
130.

'Now I want you to turn to the Second Book of Samuel,'
declares the Chaplain. 'Not the first book, the second book,
where you'll find a king who was a murderer. King David. He
killed Uriah the Hittite, because he fancied his wife Bathsheba.
He had Uriah placed in the front line of the next battle to make
sure he was killed so he could end up marrying Bathsheba.
However, God also saw what he was up to, and punished him
accordingly. Because God witnesses every murder, and will pun-
ish anyone who breaks his commandments.'

'Alleluia,' shout several of the congregation in the front three
rows.

I later learnt from the Deputy Governor that at least half the
congregation were murderers, so the Chaplain was well aware of
the audience he was playing to.

After the sermon is over the Gospel singers sing a quiet
reprise while the Chaplain asks if all those who are willing to
put their trust in God might like to come forward and sign the
pledge. A queue begins to form in front of David, and he blesses
them one by one. Once they are back in their seats, we sing the
last hymn before receiving the Chaplain's final blessing. As we
file out, I thank the Reverend before being searched – but what
could possibly change hands during the service, when they've
already searched us before we came in? I find out a week later.
We are then escorted back to our cells and locked up once again.

12 noon

At midday we're let out for Sunday lunch. There are four
different dishes on offer – turkey, beef, ham and stew. As I am
unable to tell which is which, I settle for some grated cheese

and two slices of un-margarined bread, before returning to my cell to sit at my little table and slowly nibble my cheese sandwich.

Once I've finished lunch, which takes all of five minutes, I start writing again. I continue uninterrupted for a couple of hours until Kevin returns clutching a plastic bag of goodies – two Weetabix, a carton of milk, two small green apples, a bar of soap and – his biggest triumph to date – two packets of Cup a Soup, minestrone and mushroom. I don't leave him in any doubt how grateful I am before settling down to a plastic bowl of Weetabix soaked in milk. The same bowl I'd used to shave in earlier this morning.

4.20 pm

It's not until after four has struck that I am allowed to leave the cell again and join the other prisoners for forty-five minutes in the exercise yard. I quickly learn that you take any and every opportunity – from religion to work to exercise – to make sure you get out of your cell. Once again, we're searched before being allowed to go into the yard.

Most of the inmates don't bother to walk, but simply congregate in groups and sunbathe while lounging up against the fence. Just a few of us stride purposefully round. I walk briskly because I'm already missing my daily visit to the gym. I notice that several prisoners are wearing the latest Nike or Reebok trainers. It's the one fashion statement they are allowed to make. One of the inmates joins me and shyly offers ten pages of a manuscript and asks if I would be willing to read them. He tells me that he writes three pages a day and hopes to finish the work by the time he's released in December.

I read the ten pages as I walk. He is clearly quite well

educated as the sentences are grammatically correct and he has a good command of language. I congratulate him on the piece, wish him well, and even admit that I am carrying out the same exercise myself. One or two others join me to discuss their legal problems, but as I have little knowledge of the law, I am unable to answer any of their questions. I hear my name called out on the tannoy, and return to the officer at the gate.

'Mr Peel wants to see you,' the officer says without explanation, and this time doesn't bother to search me as I am escorted to a little office in the centre of the spur. Another form needs to be filled in, as James had phoned asking if he can visit me on Friday.

'Do you want to see him?' he asks.

'Of course I do,' I reply.

'They don't all want to,' Mr Peel remarks as he fills out the form. When he has completed the task, he asks how I am settling in.

'Not well,' I admit. 'Being locked up for seventeen hours ... but I'm sure you've heard it all before.'

Mr Peel begins to talk about his job and the problems the prison service is going through. He's been a prison officer for ten years, and his basic pay is still only £24,000, which with overtime at £13.20 an hour (maximum allowed, nine hours a week) he can push up to £31,000. I didn't tell him that it's less than I pay my secretary. He then explains that his partner is also a prison officer and she carries out her full overtime stint, which means they end up with £60,000 a year between them, but don't see a lot of each other. After getting his message across, he changes the subject back to Belmarsh.

'This is only a reception prison,' he explains. 'If you're convicted and not on remand, we move you to another prison as quickly as possible. But I'm sorry to say we see the same old faces returning again and again. They aren't all bad, you know, in fact if it wasn't for drugs, particularly heroin, sixty per cent of them wouldn't even be here.'

'Sixty per cent?' I repeat.

'Yes, most of them are in for petty theft to pay for their drug habit or are part of the drug culture.'

'And can they still get hold of drugs in prison?'

'Oh yes, you'll have noticed how rudimentary the searches are. That's because prison regulations don't permit us to do any more. We know where they're hiding the drugs and every method they use to bring them in, but because of the Human Rights Act we're not always allowed to carry out a thorough enough search. Some of them are even willing to swallow plastic packets full of heroin, they're so desperate.'

'But if the packet were to burst?'

'They'll die within hours,' he says. 'One prisoner died that way last month, but you'd be surprised how many of them are still willing to risk it. Did you hear the fire alarm go off last night?'

'Yes, it woke me,' I told him.

'It was a heroin addict who'd set fire to his cell. By the time I got there he was cutting his wrist with a razor, because he wanted to suffer even more pain to help take his mind off the craving. We whisked him off to the medical wing, but there wasn't much they could do except patch him up. He'll go through exactly the same trauma again tonight, so we'll just have to mount a suicide watch and check his cell every fifteen minutes.'

A horn sounds to announce that the exercise period is over. 'I suppose you'd better get back to your cell,' he says. 'If you weren't writing a book, I can't imagine what the authorities imagine will be gained by sending you here.'

DAY 4

5.00 pm

I return to my cell and continue writing until supper. When my door is unlocked again I go down to the hotplate on the ground floor. I settle for a Thermos of hot water, an apple and a plastic bag containing tomorrow's breakfast. Back in my cell I munch a packet of crisps and with the aid of half the hot water in the Thermos make a Cup a Soup – mushroom. The cell door is slammed shut at five thirty, and will not be opened again until nine thirty tomorrow morning, by which time I will have used the other half of the water from the Thermos to take a shave, in the same bowl as I eat the soup.

I spend the next couple of hours following the Open Golf on Radio 5 Live. David Duval, an American, wins his first Open, to see his name inscribed on the silver claret jug. Colin Montgomerie and Ian Woosnam put up a spirited fight, but are not around at the seventy-second hole.

I flick over to Radio 4 to hear Steve Norris (Vice-Chairman of the Conservative Party in charge of women's affairs) telling the world he always knew I was a bad man. In the election among Party members for candidate for Mayor of London, I defeated Mr Norris by 71 per cent to 29 per cent.

I turn the radio off and read a couple of chapters of *The Moon's a Balloon*, which takes Mr Niven to Sandhurst before being commissioned into the King's Own Highlanders. I rest my head on the rock-hard pillow, and, despite the prisoners shouting from cell to cell and loud rap music coming from every corner of the block, I somehow fall asleep.

DAY 5   MONDAY 23 JULY 2001

5.53 am

The sun is shining through the bars of my window on what must be a glorious summer day. I've been incarcerated in a cell five paces by three for twelve and a half hours, and will not be let out again until midday; eighteen and a half hours of solitary confinement. There is a child of seventeen in the cell below me who has been charged with shoplifting – his first offence, not even convicted – and he is being locked up for eighteen and a half hours, unable to speak to anyone. This is Great Britain in the twenty-first century, not Turkey, not Nigeria, not Kosovo, but Britain.

I can hear the right-wingers assuring us that it will be character-building and teach the lad a lesson. What stupidity. It's far more likely that he will become antagonistic towards authority and once he's released, turn to a life of crime. This same young man will now be spending at least a fortnight with murderers, rapists, burglars and drug addicts. Are these the best tutors he can learn from?

12 noon

I am visited by a charming lady who spotted me sitting in church on Sunday. I end up asking her more questions than she asks

53

me. It turns out that she visits every prisoner who signs the pledge – I fear I didn't – and any inmate who attends chapel for the first time. She gives each prisoner a Bible and will sit and listen to their problems for hours. She kindly answers all my questions. When she leaves, I pick up my plastic tray, plastic bowl, plastic plate, plastic knife, fork and spoon, leave my cell to walk down to the hotplate for lunch.*

One look at what's on offer and once again I return to my cell empty-handed. An old lag on his way back to the top floor tells me that Belmarsh has the worst grub of any jail in Britain. As he's been a resident of seven prisons during the past twenty years, I take his word for it. An officer slams my cell door closed. It will not open again until two o'clock. I've had precisely twelve minutes of freedom during the last twenty and a half hours.

2.00 pm

After another two hours, I'm let out for Association. During this blessed release, I stop to glance at the TV in the centre of the room that's surrounded by a dozen prisoners. They're watching a cowboy film starring Ray Milland, who plays the sheriff. Normally I would flick to another channel but today it's the selection of the majority so I hang in there for ten minutes before finally giving up and moving on to the dominoes table.

An Irishman joins me and asks if I can spare him a minute. He's about five feet eight, with two scars etched across his face – one above his left eyebrow, short, the stitches still showing, and another down his right cheek, long and red. The latter I

---

* In prison, the morning meal, breakfast, is usually taken between 7.30 and 8.00, the midday meal is called dinner, and the evening meal tea. In Belmarsh, the following day's breakfast is given to you in a plastic bag when you go down to the hotplate for tea the night before.

suspect is the more recent. Despite this disfigurement, he has that soft lilt of his countrymen that I can never resist.

'I'm up in court next week,' he says.

'What for?' I ask.

'You'd rather not know,' he replies, 'but all I want to find out is, once I'm in court, am I allowed to defend myself?'

'Yes,' I tell him.

'But would it be better to give my side of the story to a barrister and then let him brief the jury?'

I consider this for a moment because during my seven-week trial I gained some experience of the legal profession. 'On balance,' I tell him, 'I would take advantage of any legal expertise on offer, rather than rely on your own cunning.' He nods and slips away. I dread meeting up with this sharp, intelligent Irishman at some later date to be told that his barrister was a fool.

I stroll back across the room to see how the film is progressing. Being a western, a gunfight to end all gunfights is just about to take place when the officer on duty shouts, 'Back to your cells.' A groan goes up, but to be fair to the duty officer, he's seated at the far end of the room and has no idea that the film only has another five minutes to run.

'The good guys win, Ray Milland gets the girl, and the baddies are all blown away,' I tell the audience assembled round the TV.

'You've seen it before?' asks one of the inmates.

'No, you stupid fucker,' says another. 'We always lose. Have you ever known it end any other way?'

Once locked back in my cell after the forty-five-minute break, I pour myself a glass of Buxton water, eat a packet of Smith's crisps and nibble away at an apple. Having finished my five-minute non-prison meal, I clean my teeth and settle down to another stint of writing.

I've written about a thousand words when I hear a key turning in the lock, always a welcome distraction because, as I've mentioned before, an open door gives you a feeling of freedom and the possibility that you might even be allowed to escape for a few minutes.

I'm greeted by a lady in civilian clothes who wears the inevitable badge – in her case, Librarian. 'Good afternoon,' I say as I rise from my place and smile. She looks surprised.

'If a prisoner asks you to sign a book, could you in future say no,' she says without bothering to introduce herself. I look puzzled; after all, I've been asked to sign books for the past twenty-five years. 'It's just that they are all library books,' she continues, 'and they're being stolen. They've now become like tobacco and phonecards, a trading item for drugs, and are worth double with your signature.'

I assure her I will not sign another library book. She nods and slams the door closed.

I continue writing, aware that the next opportunity for a break will come when we have the allocated forty-five minutes for afternoon exercise. I'm already becoming used to the routine of the door opening, lining up to be searched, and then being released into the yard. I've written about another two thousand words before the door opens again.

Having gone through the ritual, I stroll around the large square accompanied by Vincent (burglary) and another man called Mark (driving offence), who supports Arsenal. One circuit, and I discover that the only way to stop Mark boring me to death about his favourite football team is to agree with him that Arsenal, despite Manchester United's recent record, is the best team in England.

Desperate for a change of subject, I point to a sad figure

walking in front of us, the only prisoner in the yard who looks older than me.

'Poor old thing,' says Vincent. 'He shouldn't be here, but he's what's known as a bag man – nowhere to go, so he ends up in prison.'

'But what was his crime?' I ask.

'Nothing, if the truth be known. Every few weeks he throws a brick through a shop window and then hangs around until the police turn up to arrest him.'

'Why would he do that?' I ask.

'Because he's got nowhere to go and at least while he's inside the poor old sod is guaranteed a bed and three meals a day.'

'But surely the police have worked that out by now?' I suggest.

'Yes, of course they have, so they advise the magistrate to bind him over. But he's even found a way round that, because the moment the magistrate fails to sentence him, he shouts out at the top of his voice, "You're a stupid old fucker, and I'm going to throw a brick through your window tonight, so see you again tomorrow." That assures him at least another six weeks inside, which is exactly what he was hoping for in the first place. He's been sentenced seventy-three times in the past thirty years, but never for more than three months. The problem is that the system doesn't know what to do with him.'

A young black man runs past me, to the jeers of those lolling up against the perimeter fence. He is not put off, and if anything runs a little faster. He's lean and fit, and looks like a quarter-miler. I watch him, only to be reminded that my planned summer holiday at the World Athletics Championships in Edmonton with Michael Beloff has been exchanged for three weeks in Belmarsh.

'Let's get moving,' whispers Vincent. 'We want to avoid that one at any cost,' he adds, pointing to a lone prisoner walking a few paces ahead of us. Vincent doesn't speak again until we've overtaken him, and are out of earshot. He then answers my unasked question. 'He's a double murderer – his wife and her boyfriend.' Vincent goes on to describe how he killed them both. I found the details so horrific that I must confess I didn't feel able to include Vincent's words in this diary until six months after I'd left Belmarsh. If you're at all squeamish, avoid reading the next three paragraphs.

This is Vincent's verbatim description.

That bastard returned home unexpectedly in the middle of the day, to find his wife making love to another man. The man tried to escape out of the bedroom window, but was knocked out with one punch. He then tied the two of them next to each other on the bed, before going down to the kitchen. He returned a few minutes later holding a serrated carving knife with a seven-inch blade. During the next hour, he stabbed the lover eleven times making sure he was still alive before finally cutting off his balls.

Once the man had died, he climbed on the bed and raped his wife, who was still tied up next to her dead lover. At the last moment he came all over the dead man's face. He then climbed off the bed, and stared at his hysterical wife. He waited for some time before inserting the carving knife deep into her vagina. He then pulled the blade slowly up through her body.

During the trial, he told the jury that he'd killed her to prove how much he loved her. He was sentenced to life with no prospect of parole.

'Just remember to avoid him at any cost,' says Vincent. 'He'd slit your throat for a half-ounce of tobacco, and as he's going to spend the rest of his life in here, nothing can be added to his sentence whatever he gets up to.'

I feel sure he's just the sort of fellow Mr Justice Potts was hoping I'd bump into.

The hooter blasts out, the unsubtle indication that our forty-five minutes is up. We are called in, block by block, so that we can return to our individual cells in smaller groups. As I'm on Block Three, I have to hang around and wait to be called. When they call Two, I notice that the double murderer is striding purposefully towards me. I bow my head hoping he won't notice, but when I look up again, I see he's staring directly at me and still heading in my direction. I look towards the four officers standing by the gate who stiffen, while the group of black men up against the fence stare impassively on. The double murderer comes to a halt a few paces in front of me.

'Can I speak to you?' he asks.

'Yes, of course,' I reply, trying to sound as if we were casual acquaintances at a garden party.

'It's just that I would like to say how much I enjoy your books, particularly *The Prodigal Daughter*. I've been in here for eleven years and I've read everything you've written. I just wanted to let you know.' I'm speechless. 'And by the way,' he adds, 'if you want that bitch of a secretary bumped off, I'll be happy to arrange it for you.'

I really thought I was going to be sick as I watched him disappear through the gate. Thank God, into another block.

6.00 pm

I'm only locked up for an hour before the bell goes for supper. I pick up my tray and grab a tin of fruit that was donated by James – my first Listener – the night before he was transferred to Whitemoor. When I join the hotplate queue, I ask Vincent if he has a tin opener. He points to an opener attached to the wall on the far side of the room, 'But you're not allowed to open anything before you've collected your grub.' I notice that he's holding a tin of spam.

'I'll swap you half my tin of fruit for half your Spam.'

'Agreed,' he says. 'I'll bring it up to your cell as soon as I've collected my meal.'

Once again I can't find anything at the hotplate that looks even vaguely edible, and settle for a couple of potatoes.

'You ought to go for the vegetarian option,' says a voice.

I look round to see Pat. 'Mary won't be pleased when she finds out you're not eating, and let's face it, the vegetarian option is one of the few things they can't make a complete mess of.' I take Pat's advice and select a vegetable fritter. As we pass the end of the counter, another plastic bag containing tomorrow's breakfast is handed to me. 'By the way,' says Pat pointing to the man who has just served me, 'that's Peter the press, he'll wash and iron that shirt for you.'

'Thank you, Pat,' I say, and turning back to Peter add, 'My children are coming to visit tomorrow and I want to look my best for them.'

'I'll make you look as if you've just stepped out of Savile Row,' Peter says. 'I'll stop by your cell and pick up the shirt once I've finished serving breakfast.'

I move on and collect a Thermos flask of hot water from another prisoner, half for a Cup a Soup, half for shaving. As I climb the yellow iron steps back to Cell 29 on the second floor, I overhear Mark, the Arsenal supporter, having a word with Mr Tuck, the officer on duty. He's pointing out, very courteously, that there are no ethnic representatives among those selected to be Listeners, tea-boys or servers behind the hotplate, despite the fact that they make up over 50 per cent of the prison population. Mr Tuck, who strikes me as a fair man, nods his agreement, and says he'll have a word with the Governor. Whether he did or not, I have no way of knowing.*

When I arrive back on the second floor Vincent is already waiting for me. I pour half my fruit into his bowl, while he cuts his Spam into two, forking over the larger portion, which I place on the plate next to my vegetable fritter and two potatoes. He also gives me a white T-shirt, which I'm wearing as I write these words.

The cell doors are left open for about ten minutes during which time Peter the press arrives and takes away my dirty white shirt, a pair of pants and socks. 'I'll have them back to you first thing tomorrow, squire,' he promises, and is gone before I can thank him and ask what he would like in return.

My final visitor for the day is Kevin, my Listener, who tells me there's a rumour that I'm going to be moved to Block One tomorrow, where the regime is a little bit more relaxed and not quite as noisy. I'm sorry to learn this as I'm beginning to make a few friends – Kevin, James, Pat, Vincent, Peter and Mark – and am starting to get the hang of how Block Three works. Kevin sits on the end of the bed and chats as James had warned me he would; but I welcome the company, not to mention the fact that while a Listener is in the room, the door has to be left open.

Kevin had a visit this afternoon from his wife and children. He tells me his fourteen-year-old is now taller than he is, and his nine-year-old can't understand why he doesn't come home at night.

Mr Gilford, the duty officer, hovers at my cell door, a hint that even though Kevin is a Listener, it's perhaps time for him to

---

* The reason Mark feels so strongly is because tea-boys, Listeners and hotplate workers spend far longer out of their cells than the rest of us, so it's a real privilege.

move on. I ask Mr Gilford if I can empty the remains of my meal in the dustbin at the end of the landing – only one bite taken from the fritter. He nods. The moment I return, the cell door is slammed shut.

I sit on the end of the bed and begin to go through my letters. Just over a hundred in the first post, and not one of them condemning me. Amazing how the British people do not reflect the views of the press – I've kept every letter just in case my lawyers want to inspect them: three Members of Parliament, David Faber, John Gummer and Peter Lilley, and two members of the Lords, Bertie Denham and Robin Ferrers, are among those early writers. One former minister not only says how sorry he is to learn that I'm in jail, but adds that Mr Justice Potts's summing-up was a travesty of justice, and the sentence inexplicable.

I begin to make a mental list of my real friends.

5.44 am

I seem to have settled back into my usual sleep pattern. I wake around 5.30 am, rise at six, and begin my first two-hour writing session just as I would if I were in the tranquillity of my own home. I continue to write uninterrupted until eight.

I make extensive notes on what has taken place during the day, and then the following morning I pen the full script, which usually comes to about three thousand words. I also scribble a note whenever I overhear a casual remark, or a piece of information that might be forgotten only moments later.

I am just about to shave – a process I now take some considerable time over, not just because I have time, but also because I don't want to be cut to ribbons by my prison razor – when there is a bang on the cell door. My tiny window is flicked open and Ms Newsome shouts, 'Archer, you're being moved to House Block One, get your things ready.'

I should have realized by now that such a warning would be followed by at least a two-hour wait, but inexperience causes me to abandon any attempt to shave and quickly gather together my belongings. My only concern is that my children may be visiting me this afternoon and I wouldn't want them to see me unshaven.

DAY 6

I gather everything together and, as if I were returning home at the end of a holiday, I find I have far more possessions than I started out with. By the time I have stuffed everything into my large HM Prisons plastic bag, I begin to feel apprehensive about moving off Beirut to the lifers' wing.

10.07 am

My cell door is thrown open again, and I join a dozen or so prisoners who are also being transferred to Block One. I recognize one or two of them from the exercise yard. They can't resist a chorus of 'Good morning, Jeff', 'How was your breakfast, my Lord?', and 'We must be off to the posh block if you're coming with us.'

Kevin slips into the back of the line to tell me that my white shirt has been washed and pressed by Peter, and he'll have it sent over to Block One this afternoon, but I'll have to make out a new provisions list, as each house block has its own canteen.

The walk across to my new cell via several long corridors is accompanied by the usual opening and closing ceremony of double-barred gates every few yards, and when we finally arrive, we are herded into the inevitable waiting room. I've never been much good at waiting. We've only been standing around for a few minutes when a young officer, Mr Aveling, opens the door and says, 'Archer, Mr Loughnane wants to see you about reallocation.' I've only just arrived.

'They're letting you out,' shouts one of the prisoners.

'Ask if I can share a cell with you, darling,' shouts another.

'Don't pay more than the going rate,' offers a third. Prison humour.

Mr Aveling escorts me across the corridor to a large, more comfortable room by the standards I've become used to during the past few days, and introduces me to Mr Loughnane and Mr Gates. I take a seat opposite them on the other side of the desk.

'More form-filling, I'm afraid,' says Mr Loughnane almost apologetically. 'How are you settling in?' he asks. I now accept this as the standard opening to any conversation with an officer I haven't met before.

'I'm fine, except for having to be locked up in such a confined space for so many hours.'

'Were you at public school?' Mr Gates asks.

'Yes,' I reply, wondering why he asked this non sequitur.

'It's just that we find public school boys settle in far more quickly than your average prisoner.' I don't know whether to laugh or cry. 'To be honest,' he continues, 'I've already filled in most of the boxes about whether you can read or write, if you're on any drugs and how often you've been to jail. I can also confirm that you have been allocated Category D status, and will therefore be moved to an open prison in the near future.' Like 'immediately', 'near future' has a different meaning in prison. Mr Loughnane explains that first they have to locate a prison that has a vacancy, and once that has been confirmed, there will be the added problem of transport. I raise an eyebrow.

'That's always one of our biggest headaches,' Mr Loughnane explains. 'Group 4 organize all the transport between prisons, and we have to fit in with their timetable.' He then asks, 'Do you know any Category D prisons you would like to be considered for?'

'The only open prison I've ever heard of is Ford,' I tell him, 'and the one piece of information I've picked up from a former prisoner is that they have a good library.'

'Yes, they do,' confirms Mr Gates checking the prisons hand-book on the table in front of him, as if it were a Relais Chateaux

65

guide. 'We'll give them a call later this morning and check if they have any spaces available.'

I thank them both before being escorted back to the waiting room.

'Have they fixed you up with the riverside suite?' asks one prisoner.

'No,' I reply, 'but they did promise I wouldn't have to share a cell with you.'

This feeble effort is greeted by clapping and cheers, which I later learn was because I'd stood up to a man who had blown his brother's head off. I'm glad I was told this later because, let me assure you, if I'd known at the time I would have kept my mouth shut.

The door is opened again, and this time Mr Aveling tells me that the senior officer on the block wants to see me. This is greeted by more jeers and applause. 'Be careful, Jeff, he thinks you're after his job.'

I'm led to an even more comfortable room, with chairs, a desk and even pictures on the walls, to be greeted by four officers, three men and one woman. Mr Marsland, the most senior officer present, two pips on his epaulettes,* confirms the rumour that as I won't be staying long he has put me on the lifers' spur. I am obviously unable to mask my horror at the very idea, because he quickly reassures me.

'You'll find it's the most settled wing in the prison, as most of the inmates have sentences ranging between twelve and twenty-five years, and all they want is an easy life. Otherwise they'll never be considered for transfer to a B- or C-cat, let alone parole.' Yet again, exactly the opposite of what one might imagine. 'And we also have a request,' says Mr Marsland looking

---

* One pip is a senior officer, two pips a principal officer.

down at a sheet of paper. 'Mrs Williamson is running a creative-writing course, and wonders if you would be willing to address her class?'

'Of course I will,' I said. 'How many normally attend?'

'Because it's you, we think they'll be record numbers,' says Mrs Williamson, 'so it could be as many as twelve.' I haven't addressed an audience of twelve since I was the GLC candidate for Romford thirty years ago.

'One problem has arisen,' continues Mr Marsland, 'I'm afraid there are no single cells available on the lifers' spur at the moment, so you'll have to share.' My heart sinks. Will I end up with a murderer, a rapist or a drug addict, or a combination of all three? 'But we'll try to find you a sensible cell-mate,' he concludes before standing to signal that the interview is over.

I return to the waiting room and only have to hang around for a few more minutes before we are taken off to our new cells. Once again I've been put on the top floor – I think this must be for security reasons. Cell 40 is a little larger than Cell 29, where I last resided, but far from double the size, remembering that it has to accommodate two prisoners. It measures seven paces by four, rather than five by three, and up against the far wall, directly in front of the lavatory, is a small bunk bed, which one would more normally associate with a nursery.

My room-mate turns out to be Terry. Terry the writer. He is the one who approached me in the yard and asked if I would read his manuscript. He's been selected to join me because he doesn't smoke, a rarity amongst inmates, and it's a prison regulation that if you don't smoke, they can't make you share a cell with someone who does. The authorities assumed I would be aware of this rule. I wasn't.

Terry, as I have already mentioned, is halfway through writing a novel and seems pleased to discover who his cell-mate will be. I find out later why, and it's not because he wants me to help him with his syntax.

Terry is outwardly courteous and friendly, and despite my continually asking him to call me Jeffrey, he goes on addressing me as Mr Archer. We agree that he will have the top bunk and I the bottom, on account of my advanced years. I quickly discover that he's very tidy, happy to make both beds, sweep the floor and regularly empty our little plastic bucket.

I begin to unpack my cellophane bag and store my possessions in the tiny cupboard above my bed. Once we've both finished unpacking, I explain to Terry that I write for six hours a day, and hope he will understand if I don't speak to him during those set two-hour periods. He seems delighted with this arrangement, explaining that he wants to get on with his own novel. I'm about to ask how it's progressing, when the door is opened and we're joined by a prison officer who has intercepted my freshly ironed white shirt. The officer begins by apologizing, before explaining that he will have to confiscate my white shirt, because if I were to wear it, I might be mistaken for a member of the prison staff. This is the white shirt that I'd had washed and ironed by Peter the press so that I could look smart for Will and James's visit. I'm now down to one blue shirt, and one T-shirt (borrowed). He places my white shirt in yet another plastic bag for which I have to sign yet another form. He assures me that it will be returned as soon as I have completed my sentence. On his way out, he tells me my visit has been postponed for a few days.

12 noon

After a second session of writing, the cell door is opened and we are let out for Association. I join the lifers on the ground floor, which has an identical layout to House Block Three. The lifers

(23 murderers plus a handful of ABH and GBH* to make up the numbers) range in age from nineteen to fifty, and view me with considerable suspicion. Not only because I'm a Conservative millionaire, but far worse, I will only be with them for a few days before I'm dispatched to an open prison. Something they won't experience for at least another ten years. It will take a far greater effort to break down the barriers with this particular group than the young fledgeling criminals of House Block Three.

As I stroll around, I stop to glance at the TV. A man of about my age is watching Errol Flynn and David Niven in the black-and-white version of *The Charge of the Light Brigade*. I take a seat next to him.

'I'm David,' he says. 'You haven't shaved today.'

I confess my sin, and explain that I was in the process of doing so when an officer told me I would be moving.

'Understood,' said David. 'But I have to tell you, Jeffrey, you're too old for designer stubble. All the lifers shave,' he tells me. 'You've got to cling on to whatever dignity you can in a hellhole like this,' he adds, 'and a warm shower and a good shave are probably the best way to start the day.' David goes on chatting during the film as if it was nothing more than background muzak. He apologizes for not having read any of my novels, assuring me that his wife has enjoyed all of them, but he only finds time to read whenever he's in jail. I resist asking the obvious question.

'What are you reading at the moment?' I enquire.

'Ackroyd's *Life of Dickens*,' he replies. And, as if he senses my incredulity, adds, 'Mr Micawber, what a character, bit like my father to be honest, always in debt. Now remind me, what was his Christian name?'

'Wilkins,' I reply.

---

* Actual Bodily Harm and Grievous Bodily Harm.

'Just testing, Jeffrey, just testing. Actually I tried to get one of your books out of the library the other day, but they've removed them all from the shelves. A diabolical liberty, that's what I'd call it. I told them I wanted to read it, not steal the bloody thing.' I begin to notice how few prisoners use bad language in front of me. One of the other inmates, who has been watching the TV, leans across and asks me if the story's true. I can just about recall Tennyson's poem of the gallant six hundred, and I'm fairly certain Errol Flynn didn't ride through the enemy lines, and thrust a sword into the heart of their leader.

'Of course he did,' says David, 'it was in his contract.'

On this occasion we do get to see the closing titles, because the duty officer has checked what time the film finishes. He prefers not to have thirty or forty disenchanted lifers on his hands.

At two we're invited to return to our cells for lock-up. This invitation takes the form of an officer bellowing at the top of his voice. On arrival, I find another 200 letters waiting for me on the bottom bunk. All of them have been opened, as per prison regulations, to check they do not contain any drugs, razor blades or money. Reading every one of them kills another couple of hours while you're 'banged up'. I'm beginning to think in prison jargon.

The public seems genuinely concerned about my plight. Many of them comment on the judge's summing-up and the harshness of the sentence, while others point out that bank robbers, paedophiles and even those charged with manslaughter often get off with a two- or three-year sentence. The recurring theme is 'What does Mr Justice Potts have against you?' I confess I don't know the answer to that question, but what cannot be denied is that I asked my barrister, Nick Purnell, on the third, fourth and seventh days of the trial to speak to the judge privately in chambers about his obvious prejudice, and request a retrial. However, my silk advised against this approach, on the grounds that it would only turn the whole trial into an all-out battle between the two of us. Lest you might think I am making this all up conveniently after the event, I also confided my fears to the Honourable Michael Beloff QC, Gilbert Gray QC and Johnnie Nutting QC during the trial.

It isn't until the second hour that I come across a letter demanding that I should apologize to all those I had let down. The next letter in the pile is from Mary. I read it again and again. She begins by remarking that she couldn't remember when she had last written to me. She reminds me that she is off to Strathclyde University this morning to chair the summer school on solar energy, accompanied by the world's press and my son Will. Thank God for Will. He's been a tower of strength. At the end of next week, she flies to Dresden to attend another conference, and has sent me a parcel which with any luck should arrive by the weekend. I miss her and the children, of course I do, but above anything I hope it won't be too long before the press become bored with me and allow Mary to carry on with her life.

When I come to the end of the letters, Terry helps me put them into four large brown envelopes so they can be sent on to Alison, my PA, in order that everyone who has taken the trouble to write receives a reply. While Terry is helping me, he begins to tell me his life story and how he ended up being in jail. He's not a lifer, which is perhaps another reason they asked him if he was willing to share a cell with me.

Terry has been in prison twice, graduating via Borstal and a remand centre. He began sniffing solvents as a child, before moving on to cannabis by the age of twelve. His first offence was robbing a local newsagent because he needed money for his drug habit. He was sentenced to two years and served one. His second charge was for robbing a jeweller's in Margate of £3,000 worth of goods for which he hoped to make around £800 from a London fence. The police caught him red-handed (his words), and he was sentenced to five years. He was twenty-two at the time, and served three and a half years of that sentence before being released.

Terry had only been out for seven months when he robbed an optician's – designer goods, Cartier, Calvin Klein and Christian Dior, stolen to order. This time he was paid £900 in cash, but arrested a week later. The fingerprints on the shop window he put his fist through matched his, leaving the police with only one suspect. The judge sentenced him to another five years.

Terry hopes to be released in December of this year. Prison, he claims, has weaned him off drugs and he's only thankful that he's never tried heroin. Terry is nobody's fool, and I only hope that when he gets out he will not return for a third time. He swears he won't, but a prison officer tells me that two-thirds of repeat offenders are back inside within twelve months.

'We have our regulars just like any Blackpool hotel, except we don't charge for bed and breakfast.'

Terry is telling me about his mother, when suddenly there is a wild commotion of screaming and shouting that reverberates throughout the entire block. It's the first time I'm glad that my cell door is locked. The prisoners in Block One are yelling at a man who is being escorted to the medical centre on the far side of the yard. I remember it well.

'What's all that about?' I ask as I stare out of our cell window.

'He's a nonce,' Terry explains.

'Nonce?'

'Prison slang for a nonsense merchant, a paedophile. If he'd been on this block we would have jugged him long ago.'

'Jugged him?'

'A jug of boiling hot water,' Terry explains, 'mixed with a bag of sugar to form a syrup. Two cons would hold him down while the liquid is poured slowly over his face.'

'My God, that must be horrific.'

'First the skin peels off your face and then the sugar dissolves, so you end up disfigured for the rest of your life – no more than he deserves,' Terry adds.

'Have you ever witnessed that?' I ask.

'Three times,' he replies matter-of-factly. 'One nonce, one drug dealer, and once over an argument about someone who hadn't returned a two-pound phonecard.' He pauses before adding, 'If they were to put him on this block, he'd be dead within twenty-four hours.'

I'm terrified, so I can only wonder what sort of fear they live in. The moment the prisoner disappears into the medical centre, the shouting and yelling stops.

4.00 pm

The cell door is at last unlocked and we are allowed out into the exercise yard. On my first circuit, about two hundred yards, I'm joined by a young prisoner – come to think of it, everyone is young except for me and David. His name is Nick, and if it weren't for his crooked front teeth and broken nose, he would be a good-looking man. He's been in prison for the past fourteen years, and he's only thirty-three, but he hopes to be out in four years' time as long as he can beat his latest rap.

'Your latest rap?' I repeat.

'Yeah, they've been trying to pin arson on me after what I got up to in Durham, but they've got no proof that I set fire to my cell, so they'll have to drop the charge.' He's joined by another lifer who has just completed four of his eighteen years.

There seems to be a completely different attitude among the lifers. They often say, 'Don't bother to count the first six years.' They acknowledge they won't be out next week, next month, or even next year, and have settled for a long spell of prison life. Most of them treat me with respect and don't indulge in clever or snide remarks.

On the next circuit I'm joined by Mike (armed robbery), who tells me that he listened to Ted Francis and Max Clifford on the radio last night, and adds that the boys just can't wait for one of them to be sent to prison. 'We don't like people who stitch up their mates – especially for money.' I stick assiduously to Nick Purnell's advice and make no comment.

When I return to the cell, Terry is about to go down for supper. I tell him I just can't face it, but he begs me to join him because tonight it's pineapple upside-down pudding, and that's his favourite. I join him and go through the ritual of selecting a couple of burnt mushrooms in order to lay my hands on an extra upside-down pudding.

By the time I get back to the cell, Terry is sweeping the room and cleaning the washbasin. I've been lucky to be shacked up with someone who is so tidy, and hates anything to be out of place. Terry sits on the bed munching his meal, while I read through what I've penned that day. Once Terry's finished, he washes his plate, knife, fork and spoon before stacking them neatly on the floor in the corner. I continue reading my script while he picks up a Bible. He turns to the Book of Hebrews, which I confess I have never read, and studies quietly for the next hour.

Once I've completed my work for the day, I return to reading *The Moon's a Balloon*, which I put down just after ten when war has been declared. The pillows are a little softer than those on Block Three, for which I am grateful.

DAY 7   WEDNESDAY 25 JULY 2001

5.17 am

'Fuck off,' cries a voice so loud it wakes me.

It's a few moments before I realize that it's Terry shouting in his sleep. He mumbles something else which I can't quite decipher, before he wakes with a start. He climbs out of bed, almost as if he's unaware there's someone in the bunk below him. I don't stir, but open my eyes and watch carefully. I'm not frightened; although Terry has a past record of violence, I've never seen any sign of it. In fact, despite the use of bad language in his novel, he never swears in front of me – at least not when he's awake.

Terry walks slowly over to the wall and places his head in the corner like a cat who thinks he's about to die. He doesn't move for some time, then turns, picks up a towel by the basin, sits down on the plastic chair and buries his head in the towel. Desperate and depressed. I try to imagine what must be going through his tortured mind. He slowly raises his head and stares at me, as if suddenly remembering that he's not alone.

'Sorry, Mr Archer,' he says. 'Did I wake you?'

'It's not important,' I reply. 'Do you want to talk about it?'

'It's a recurring nightmare,' he says, 'but for some unexplainable reason it's been worse for the past couple of weeks. When I was a kid,' he pauses, no doubt considering whether to confide in me, 'my stepfather used to beat me and my mum with a leather strap, and I've suddenly started having nightmares about it all these years later.'

'How old were you at the time?' I ask.

'About six, but it carried on until I was sixteen, when my mum died.'

'How did your mother die?' I ask. 'After all, she can't have been that old?'

'It's all a bit of a mystery,' Terry says quietly. 'All I know for certain is that they found her body in the front room by the grate, and then my stepfather buggered off to Brighton with my stepsister.' I have a feeling that Terry knows only too well what and who caused his mother's death, but he isn't yet willing to impart that information. After all, he's well aware I'm writing a daily diary.

'So what happened to you when he disappeared off to Brighton?'

'I was taken into care, followed by Borstal, remand home and finally jail – a different sort of education to yours.' How can those of us who have had a comparatively normal upbringing begin to understand what this young man has been through – is going through?

'Sorry,' he repeats, and then climbs back onto the top bunk, and is asleep again within minutes.

I climb out of bed, clean my teeth, rub a cold flannel over my face and then settle down to write for the first session of the day. At this early hour, all the other prisoners are asleep, or at least I assume they are, because not a sound is coming from the surrounding cells. Even the early-morning patrol of barking Alsatians doesn't distract me any longer.

In London I live near a railway track that winds its way into

Waterloo, but I am never woken by the late-night or early-morning trains. In prison, it's rap music, inmates hollering at each other, and Alsatians that don't disturb a lifer's dreams. Once I've completed my two-hour session, I begin the lengthy process of shaving.

Although my life is beginning to fall into a senseless routine, I hope to at least break it up today by going to the gym. I've put my name down for the 10 am to 11 am session this morning, as I'm already missing my daily exercise.

9.06 am

Just after nine, the cell door is opened and my weekly twelve pounds fifty pence worth of canteen provisions are passed over to me by a lady in a white coat. I thank her, but she doesn't respond. I sit on the end of my bed, unpack each item one by one. I settle down to enjoy a bowl of cornflakes swimming in fresh milk. This is the meal I would normally have in my kitchen at home, an hour before going to the gym. I'm used to a disciplined, well-ordered life, but it's no longer self-discipline because someone else is giving the orders.

10.00 am

I'm pacing up and down the cell waiting for the gym call when a voice bellows out from below, 'Gym is cancelled.' My heart sinks and I stare out of the barred window, wondering why. When the door is eventually opened for Association, Derek, known as Del Boy, who runs the hotplate and seems to have a free rein of the block, appears outside my door.

'Why was gym cancelled?' I ask.

'A con has got out onto the roof via a skylight in the gym,' he explains. Result – gym closed until further notice and will not open again until security has double-checked every possible exit and the authorities consider it a safe area again. He grins, enjoying his role as the prison oracle.

'Anything else I can help you with?' Del Boy enquires.

'Bottled water and an A4 writing pad,' I reply.

'They'll be with you before the hour has chimed, squire.'

I've already learnt not to ask what myriad of deals will have to be carried out to achieve this simple request. James had warned me on my first day about the prison term 'double-bubble', meaning certain favours have to be repaid twice over. During Association yesterday evening, I witnessed Derek cut a rolled-up cigarette in half and then pass it over to another prisoner. This was on a Tuesday, and the hapless inmate knew he wouldn't be able to repay the debt until today, when he would have his next canteen. But his craving was so great that he accepted, knowing that he would have to give Del Boy a whole cigarette in return, or he could never hope to strike up another bargain with him – or anyone else, for that matter.

11.10 am

It must have been a few minutes after eleven when my cell door is yanked open again to reveal Mr Loughnane. Just the sight of him lifts my spirits. He tells me that he has spoken to his opposite number at Ford Open Prison, who will have to refer the matter to the Governor, as he doesn't have the authority to make the final decision.

'How long do you expect that will take?' I ask.

'Couple of days at the most. He'll probably come back to me on Friday, and when he does, I'll be in touch with Group 4.' This simple transaction would take the average businessman a couple of hours at most. For the first time in years, I'm having to move at someone else's pace.

1.00 pm

We are all sent off to work. I'm down on the register under 'workshops' where I will have to pack breakfast bags that will eventually end up in other prisons. My salary will be 50p an hour. New Labour's minimum-wage policy hasn't quite trickled down to convicted felons. The truth is we're captive labour. I'm about to join the chain gang when another prison officer, Mr Young, asks me to wait behind until the others have left for the work area. He returns a few minutes later, to tell me that I've received so much registered mail they have decided to take me to it, rather than bring the stack to me.

Another long walk in a different direction, even more opening and closing of barred gates, by which time I have learnt that Mr Young has been in the prison service for eleven years, his annual basic pay is £24,000, and it's quite hard, if not impossible, to find somewhere to live in London on that salary.

When we arrive at reception, two other officers are standing behind a counter in front of rows and rows of cluttered wooden shelves. Mr Pearson removes thirty-two registered letters and parcels from a shelf behind him and places them on the counter. He starts to open them one by one in front of me – another prison regulation. The two officers then make a little pile of Bibles and books and another of gifts which they eventually place in a plastic bag, and once I've signed the requisite form, hand them all across to me.

'Peach,' says Mr Pearson, and another prisoner steps forward to have a parcel opened in front of him. It's a pair of the latest Nike trainers, which have been sent in by his girlfriend.

Both clutching onto our plastic bags, we accompany Mr Young back to Block One. On the way, I apologize to Peach – I never did find out his first name – for keeping him waiting.

'No problem,' he says. 'You kept me out of my cell for nearly an hour.'

Mr Young continues to tell us about some of the other problems the prison service is facing. We are onto staff benefits and shiftwork when an alarm goes off, and officers appear running towards us from every direction. Mr Young quickly unlocks the nearest waiting room and bundles Peach and myself inside, locking the door firmly behind us. We stare through the windows as officers continue rushing past us, but we have no way of finding out why. A few moments later, a prisoner, held down by three officers and surrounded by others, is dragged off past us in the opposite direction. One of the officers is pushing the prisoner's head down, while another keeps his legs bent so that when he passes us he leaves an impression of a marionette controlled by invisible strings. Peach tells me that it's known as being 'bent up' or 'twisted up', and is part of the process of 'control and restraint'.

'Control and restraint?'

'The prisoner will be dragged into a strip cell and held down while his clothes are cut off with a pair of scissors. He's then put in wrist locks, before they bend his legs behind his back. Finally they put a belt around his waist that has handcuffs on each side, making it impossible for him to move his arms or legs.'

'And then what?'

'They'll take him off to segregation,' Peach explains. 'He'll be put into a single cell that consists of a metal sink, metal table and metal chair all fixed to the wall, so he can't smash anything up.'

'How long will they leave him there?'

'About ten days,' Peach replies.

'Have you ever been in segregation?' I ask.

'No,' he says firmly, 'I want to get out of this place as quickly as possible, and that's the easiest way to be sure your sentence is lengthened.'

Once the commotion has died down, Mr Young returns to unlock the door and we continue our journey back to the cells as if nothing had happened.

Each block has four spurs, which run off from the centre like a Maltese cross. In the middle of the cross is an octangular glass office, known as the bubble, which is situated on the centre of the three floors. From this vantage point, the staff can control any problems that might arise. As we pass the bubble, I ask the duty officer what happened.

'One of the prisoners,' he explains, 'has used threatening and abusive language when addressing a woman officer.' He adds no further detail to this meagre piece of information.

Once back in my cell, Terry tells me that the prisoner will be put on report and be up in front of the Governor tomorrow morning. He also confirms that he'll probably end up with ten days in solitary.

'Have you ever been in segregation?' I ask him.

'Three times,' he admits. 'But I was younger then, and can tell you, I don't recommend it, even as an experience for your diary. By the way,' he adds, 'I've just phoned my dad. The *Daily Express* have been onto him offering a grand for a photo of me – *the con Jeffrey has to live with* – and they've offered him another thousand if he'll give them all the details of my past criminal record. He told them to bugger off, but he says they just won't go away. They sounded disappointed when he told them I wasn't a murderer.'

'You will be by the time the Sunday editions come out,' I promise him.

DAY 7

2.00 pm

Another officer opens the door to tell us that our afternoon Association will be cut short because the prison staff are holding a meeting. Terry tells the officer who passes on this information that any staff meeting should be held when we are banged up, not during Association. He makes a fair point, but all the officer says is, 'It's not my decision,' and slams the door.

2.02 pm

What is almost impossible to describe in its full horror is the time you spend *banged up*. So please do not consider this diary to be a running commentary, because I would only ask you to think about the endless hours in between. Heaven knows what that does to lifers who can see no end to their incarceration, and do not have the privilege of being able to occupy their time writing. In my particular case, there is Hope, a word you hear prisoners using all the time. They hope that they'll win their case, have their sentence cut, be let out on parole, or just be moved to a single cell. For me, as a Category D prisoner, I simply hope to be transferred to Ford Open Prison as soon as possible. But God knows what a lifer hopes for, and I resolve to try and find out during the next few days.

4.30 pm

Association. At last the cell door is opened for an extended period of time – forty-five minutes. When I walk down to join the other inmates on the ground floor, Paul (murder) hands me a book of first-class stamps, and asks for nothing in return. He either has no one to write to, or perhaps can't write. 'I hear you're having a postage problem,' is all he says, and walks away. I do not explain that my PA is dealing with all my letters, and therefore I have no postage problem, because it would only belittle such a thoughtful gesture.

During Association I notice that the high barred gates at the end of the room lead onto a larger outer area which has its own television, pool table, and more comfortable chairs. But I'm not permitted to enter this hallowed territory as you can only leave the restricted area if you're an *enhanced* prisoner.

There are three levels of prisoner: basic, standard and enhanced. Every inmate begins their sentence as standard – in the middle. This leaves you the chance to go up or down, and that decision depends solely on your behaviour. Someone who wishes to take on more responsibility, like being a Listener, a tea-boy or a cleaner, will quickly be promoted to enhanced status and enjoy the privileges that go with it. However, anyone who attacks a prison officer or is caught taking drugs will be downgraded to basic. And these things matter when it comes to your standard of living in prison, and later when the authorities consider your parole, and possible early release.

Terry, my cell-mate, hates authority and refuses to go along with the system, so spends his life bobbing up and down between basic and standard. Derek 'Del Boy' Bicknell, on the other hand, took advantage of the system and quickly became enhanced. But then he is bright, and well capable of taking on responsibility. He already has the free run of the ground floor and in fact never seems to be in his cell. I hope by now you have a picture in your mind of Del Boy, because he's a six-foot, twenty-stone West Indian who wears a thin gold chain around his neck, a thicker one around his right wrist, and sports the latest designer watch. He also wears a fashionable tracksuit and Nike shoes. Come to think of it, I'm the only prisoner who still wears a shirt, but if I were to remain here for any length of time, I would also end up wearing a tracksuit.

5.30 pm

Supper, called tea, is being served, so I return to my cell to collect my plastic tray and plate. Tonight it's egg and bacon and I'm just too hungry to say no. The egg has a solid yolk and the greasy bacon is fatty, curling and inedible. I drink a mug of Highland Spring water (a trade for two autographs on birthday cards) and finish the meal with a bowl of Cup a Soup (minestrone, 24p). At the next election no one will be able to accuse me of not knowing the price of goods in the supermarket, not to mention their true value.

Terry cleans our utensils before we return to Association on the ground floor, where I find Del Boy running a card school at the other end of the room. Why am I not surprised? He beckons me to join them. The game is made up of four lifers who are playing Kaluki. I watch a couple of hands while trying to keep an eye on the phone queue, as I'm hoping to speak to Mary. She should have returned from her day at Strathclyde University and be back in her hotel. By now you will have realized that she can't call me.

Paul (murder and stamps) announces he needs to phone his girlfriend and suggests I take over his hand while he joins the queue.

'Jeff's got to be an improvement on you,' says Derek as Paul rises to depart.

I lose the first hand badly, survive the second, and win the third. Thankfully, before Del Boy starts dealing the fourth, Paul returns.

'His Lordship's not bad,' says Derek, 'not bad at all.' I'm slowly being accepted.

The queue for the two phones doesn't seem to diminish, so I spend some time talking to a young lifer called Michael (murder). He's very pale-skinned, extremely thin, and covered in tattoos, with needle tracks up and down his arms. He invites me into his cell, and shows me a picture of his wife and child. By the time Michael is released from prison, his eight-month-old daughter will have left school, probably be married and have children of her own. In fact this twenty-two-year-old boy may well be a grandfather by the time he's released.

When I leave Michael's cell to rejoin the others I spot Ms Roberts, the Deputy Governor, who came to visit me when I was on the medical wing. She is surrounded by lifers. Ms Roberts has a real gift for putting these desperate men at ease.

I finally give up and join the phone queue, aware that we are fast approaching lock-up. When at last I make the one spare phone out of two a lifer who is on the other line leans over to warn me that any conversations made on these phones are tape recorded by the police. I thank him, but can't imagine what they would find of interest eavesdropping on a chat with my wife. A hotel operator answers the call and puts me through to her room. The phone rings and rings.

7.00 pm

I return to my cell to be faced with another mountain of mail. Terry helps by taking them out of their envelopes before placing them in piles, cards on one side, letters on the other, while I continue to go over the script I've written that day. Terry asks if he can keep one or two of the cards as a memento. 'Only if they have no address,' I tell him, 'as it's still my intention to reply to every one of them.'

Once I've finished correcting my daily script, I turn my attention to the letters. Like my life, they are falling into a pattern of their own, some offering condolences on my mother's death, others kindness and support. Many continue to comment on Mr Justice Potts's summing-up, and the harshness of the sentence. I am bound to admit they bring back one's faith in one's fellow men ... and women.

Alison, my PA, has written to say that I am receiving even more correspondence by every post at home, and she confirms that they are also running at three hundred to one in support. I hand one of the letters up to Terry. It's from his cousin who's read in the papers that we're sharing a cell. Terry tells me that he's serving a life sentence in Parkhurst for murder. My cell-mate adds they haven't spoken to each other for years. And it was only a couple of hours ago I was feeling low because I haven't managed to speak to Mary today.

DAY 8   THURSDAY 26 JULY 2001

5.03 am

I've slept for seven hours. When I wake, I begin to think about my first week in prison. The longest week of my life. For the first time, I consider the future and what it holds for me. Will I have to follow the path of two of my heroes, Emma Hamilton and Oscar Wilde, and choose to live a secluded life abroad, unable to enjoy the society that has been so much a part of my very existence?

Will I be able to visit old haunts – the National Theatre, Lord's, Le Caprice, the Tate Gallery, the UGC Cinema in Fulham Road – or even walk down the street without people's only thought being 'There's the man who went to jail for perjury'? I can't explain to every one of them that I didn't get a fair trial. It's so unlike me to be introspective or pessimistic, but when you're locked up in a cell seven paces by four for hour upon hour every day, you begin to wonder if anyone out there even knows you're still alive.

10.00 am

Mr Highland, a young officer, unlocks my cell door and tells me I have a legal visit at ten thirty. I ask if I might be allowed to take a shower and wash my hair.

'No,' he says. 'Use the washbasin.' Only the second officer to be offhand since I've arrived. I explain that it's quite hard to have a shower in a washbasin. He tells me that I've got an 'attitude' problem, and says that if I go on like this, he'll have to put me on report. It feels like being back at school at the wrong end of your life.

I shave and clean myself up as best I can before being escorted to yet another part of the building so that I can meet up with my lawyers. I am deposited in a room about eight foot by eight, with windows in all four walls; even lawyers have been known to bring in drugs for their clients. There's a large oblong table in the centre of the room, with six chairs around it. A few moments later I'm joined by Nick Purnell QC and his junior Alex Cameron, who are accompanied by my solicitor, Ramona Mehta. Nick takes me slowly through the process of appeal against conviction and sentence. He's fairly pessimistic about conviction, despite there being a considerable amount of evidence of the judge's bias when summing up, but he says only those in the court room will remember the emphasis and exaggeration Potts put on certain words when he addressed the jury. The judge continually reminded the jurors that I hadn't given evidence, and, holding up Mrs Peppiatt's small diary not my large office diary, repeatedly remarked that 'no one has denied this is a real diary'. He didn't point out to the jury, however, that even if that diary had appeared in the original trial, it wouldn't have made any material difference.

On the subject of sentence, Nick Purnell is more confident, as several leading members of the Bar have made it clear that they consider four years to be not only harsh, but unjust. And the public seem to be universally in agreement with the professionals. Reduction of sentence can make a great difference, because any conviction of four years or more requires a decision by the Parole Board before you can be set free. Any sentence of less than four years, even by one day, means you are automatically released after serving half your sentence, assuming you've been a model prisoner. You're also eligible for tagging, which knocks off another two months, when you are restricted to your 'chosen place of residence' between the hours of seven pm and seven am the following morning.*

We go on to discuss whether this is the right time to issue a writ against Emma Nicholson for hinting that the millions of pounds I helped raise for the Kurds didn't reach them, with the twisted implication that some of the money must therefore have ended up in my pocket. Nick points out that Sir Nicholas Young, the Chief Executive of the Red Cross, has come to my defence, and even the *Evening Standard* is saying I have no case to answer. Alex tells me that several articles are now being written in support of my position, including one by Trevor Kavanagh in the *Sun*. He also points out that the *Daily Telegraph* had a tilt at Max Hastings.

I tell Nick that I want to issue a writ against Ted Francis to recover the £12,000 I loaned him, and for claiming that over twenty years ago he'd seen a Nigerian prostitute climbing out of my bedroom window. This is quite an achievement as Francis and I stayed at different hotels and my room was on the top floor. I do hope the poor girl was a member of the Lagos mountain rescue team.

My legal team understand my anger, but want to wait until the dust has settled. I reluctantly agree, but remain unconvinced. I can't help remembering that when I complained to Nick about

---

* For example, if my sentence was reduced by one year, from four to three, I would end up only serving sixteen months and be released on 19 November 2002, whereas with a four-year sentence, the earliest I could hope to be released would be 19 July 2003.

DAY 8

Mr Justice Potts's prejudiced attitude during the pre-trial hearings and the trial itself, he advised me against raising the matter with the judge in chambers, saying it would only exacerbate the problem.

On the hour I leave them to return to their world, while I am escorted back to mine.

12 noon

I take one look at what they're offering at the hotplate for lunch, and return to my cell with an empty plastic plate. I add a packet of crisps to my opened tin of Spam, before pouring myself a mug of cranberry juice topped up with Highland Spring. My supplies are already running low.

2.00 pm

Mr Weedon comes to my cell to let me know that I have a personal visit at three o'clock.

'Who?' I enquire.

He checks his list. 'William and James Archer.'

I am about to suggest it might have been more considerate of someone to warn me yesterday rather than tell me a few minutes before my sons are due to arrive. However, as Mr Highland has already threatened to place me on report for such insolence, I decide to keep my counsel.

3.00 pm

Over eighty prisoners from all four blocks are streaming towards the visitors' area. On the long walk to the other side of the building, I come across some inmates from my short stay on

House Block Three. It's rather like meeting up with old school chums. 'How are you?' 'What have you been up to?' 'Have you met up with . . .?' When we arrive in the waiting area, the search is far more rigorous than usual. Del Boy had already warned me that this is the one time the staff are nervous about the transfer of money, drugs, blades, knives, even guns, and anything else that might be passed from a relation or family friend on to a prisoner. I am pleased to discover that my own search is fairly cursory. After the search, I am asked to place a yellow sash over my shoulder so I look like a child about to go on a bike ride. This is to indicate that I'm a prisoner, so that I can't stroll out with my sons once the visit is over. I'm bound to say that I find this tiny act humiliating.

I'm then ushered into a room about the size of a large gymnasium. Chairs are set out in five long rows marked A to E. I report to a desk that is raised three or four feet above the ground, and another officer checks his list and then tells me to go to C11. All the prisoners sit on the right-hand side, opposite their visitors who sit on the left. There is a small, low table in between us which is screwed to the floor, and is meant to keep you apart. There is also a balcony above us that overlooks the whole room, with even more officers staring down on the proceedings to see if they can spot anything being passed across the tables below them. They are assisted by several CCTV cameras. A notice on the walls states that the tapes can be used as evidence for a further prosecution, and in capitals adds: THIS APPLIES TO BOTH PRISONERS AND THEIR VISITORS.

I walk down three rows to find William sitting on his own. He jumps up and gives me a big hug, and I'm reminded just how much I've missed him. James, he tells me, is at the canteen purchasing my favourite beverage. He appears a few minutes later, carrying a tray of Diet Cokes and several KitKats. The boys laugh when I pull all three Cokes towards my side of the table, and make no attempt to offer them even a stick of the KitKat.

Will begins by telling me about Mary's visit to Strathclyde University, where she made a short statement to the press before delivering her lecture. She began by remarking that it was the largest turnout she had ever managed for a lecture on quantum solar-energy conversion.

Will is not surprised to learn that I have received over a thousand letters and cards in the first few days at Belmarsh, and he tells me there are almost three times that number back at the flat. Support is coming in from every quarter, James adds, including thoughtful statements from John Major and George Carey.

'Alison has had a list typed up,' my younger son continues, 'but they wouldn't allow me to bring anything into the visits room, so I'll have it posted on to you tomorrow.'

This news gives me such a lift, and makes me feel guilty that I had ever doubted my friends would stand by me.

I alert the two boys to the fact that I am writing a day-to-day diary, and will need to see my agent, Jonathan Lloyd, my publisher, Victoria Barnsley, and my editor, Robert Lacey, fairly soon, but, as I am only allowed one personal visit every two weeks, I don't want to see anyone other than the family until I've been moved to an open prison.

Will tells me that he's already booked himself in for two weeks' time, but hopes I will have been transferred to somewhere like Ford long before then. Because I've not been reading any newspapers or listening to the news, as I'm heartily sick of inaccurate stories about myself and what I'm up to at Belmarsh, Jamie brings me up to date on the battle for the Tory Party leadership. He reports that the polls clearly indicate that the people who deserted the Conservatives at the last election want Ken Clarke, while the party membership favours Iain Duncan

Smith. I like and admire both men, though neither is a close friend. However, it doesn't take a massive intellect to work out that if we hope to win the next election, or at least make a large enough dent in the government's majority to ensure that opinion-formers believe we can win the following election, it might be wise to take some notice of the electorate's views as to who should be our leader.

I consider dropping Ken a note, but realize it may not help his cause.

Will goes on to tell me that Michael Beloff QC, Gilbert Gray QC and Johnnie Nutting QC are in regular touch with my legal team. Gilly wondered if Potts's animosity had been aimed at Nick Purnell, as it's the talk of the Bar that he lost his temper with Nick on several occasions during the pre-trial and trial itself, but never once in front of the jury.

'No,' I tell them, 'it was nothing to do with Nick. It was entirely personal.'

I'm momentarily distracted by an attractive young woman sitting directly in front of me in row B. A prisoner with his back to me is leaning across the table and kissing her. I remember being told by Kevin that this was the most common way of passing drugs. I watch more carefully and decide this is about sex, pure animal sex, and has nothing to do with drugs.

James tells me about the film he and Nod (Nadhim Zahawi, a Kurdish friend) enjoyed on Sunday evening, *Rush Hour 2*, which in normal circumstances I would have seen with them.

'Don't worry,' he adds. 'We're keeping a list of all the films you would have enjoyed, so that you can eventually see them on video.' I don't like the sound of the word 'eventually'.

I talk to Will about when he expects to return to America and continue with his work as a documentary cameraman. He tells me that he will remain in England while his mother is so unsettled and feels in such need of him. How lucky I am to be blessed with such a family.

An announcement is made over the tannoy to inform us that all visitors must now leave. Have we really had an hour together? All round the room a great deal of kissing commences before friends and family reluctantly depart. The prisoners have to remain in their places until the last visitor has been signed out and left the room. I spend my time glancing up and down the rows. The man whose kiss had been so overtly sexual now has his head bowed in his hands. I wonder just how long his sentence is, and what age he and his girlfriend will be by the time he's released from prison.

When the last visitor has left, we all file back out of the room; once again my search is fairly cursory. I never discover what the other prisoners are put through, though. Del Boy tells me later that if they've picked up anything suspicious on the video camera, it's a full strip-search, plus sniffer dogs.

On the way back to my cell, a Block Three prisoner tells me he will be going home next month, having completed his sentence. He adds that he had a visit from his wife who is sticking by him, but if he's ever sentenced again, she's made it clear that she'll leave him.

I'm only a few yards from my cell door when Mr Weedon tells me that the education officer wants to see me. I turn round and he escorts me up to the middle floor.

The education officer is dressed in a smart brown suit. He stands up when I enter the room and shakes me by the hand.

'My name's Peter Farrell,' he says. 'I see you've put yourself down for education.'

'Yes,' I confirm. 'I was rather hoping it would give me a chance to use the library.'

'Yes, it will,' says Mr Farrell. 'But I wonder if I could ask you to assist us with those prisoners who are learning to read and write, as I'm rather short-staffed at the moment?'

'Of course,' I reply.

'You'll get a pound an hour,' he adds with a grin.

We talk for some time about the fact that there are a number of bright people among the prisoners, especially the lifers, some of whom would be quite capable of sitting for an Open University degree. 'My biggest problem,' he explains, 'is that while the inmates can earn ten to twelve pounds a week in the workshops dropping teabags, jam and sugar into plastic containers, they only receive six pounds fifty a week if they sign up for education. So I often lose out on some potentially able students for the sake of tobacco money.'

My God, there are going to be some speeches I will have to make should I ever return to the House of Lords.

There is a knock on the door, and Mr Marsland, the senior officer, comes in to warn me that it's almost time for my talk to the lifers on creative writing.

4.30 pm

The lecture is set up in one of the waiting rooms and is attended by twelve prisoners serving life sentences plus two officers to keep an eye on proceedings. There are two types of life sentence, mandatory and discretionary, but all that matters to a lifer is the tariff that has been set by the judge at their trial.

I begin my talk by telling the lifers that I didn't take up writing until I was thirty-four, after leaving Parliament and facing bankruptcy; so I try to assure them that you can begin a new career at any age. Proust, I remind them, said we all end up doing the thing we're second best at.

Once I've finished my short talk, the first two questions fired at me are about writing a novel, but I quickly discover that the other inmates mostly want to know how I feel about life behind bars and what changes I would make.

'I've only been inside for eight days,' I keep reminding them.

I try valiantly to parry their questions, but Mr Marsland and his deputy soon have to come to my rescue when the subject changes to how the prison is run, and in particular their complaints about lock-up times, food, no ice and wages. These all seem to be fair questions, though nothing to do with writing. The officers try to answer their queries without prevarication and both have so obviously given considerable thought to inmates' problems. They often sympathize, but appear to have their hands tied by regulations, bureaucracy and lack of money.

One prisoner called Tony, who seems not only to be bright but to have a real grasp of figures, discusses the £27 million budget that Belmarsh enjoys, right down to how much it costs to feed a prisoner every day. I will never forget the answer to that question – £1.27 is allocated for three meals per prisoner per day.

'Then the caterers must be making a pound a day off every one of us,' Tony retorts.

The meeting goes on well beyond the scheduled hour, and it's some time before one of the prisoners, Billy Little who hails from Glasgow, actually asks another question about writing. Do I use my novels to expound any particular political prejudice? No, I reply firmly, otherwise I'd have very few readers. Billy is a left-winger by upbringing and persuasion and argues his case well. He finds a great deal of pleasure in giving me a hard time and making me feel ill at ease with the other prisoners. By the end of a heated exchange, he is at least listening to my point of view.

On the way back to the cells, Billy tells me he's written a short story and some poetry. He asks if I would be willing to read them and offer an opinion; a sentence I usually dread when I'm on the outside. He nips into his cell on the ground floor, extracts some sheets of paper from a file and passes them over to me. I leave him to find Derek 'Del Boy' Bicknell waiting for me outside. He warns me that Terry, my cell-mate, has been talking to the press, and to be wary of saying anything to him.

'Talking to the press?'

'Yeah, the screws caught him on the phone to the *Sun*. I'm told that the going rate for an exclusive with anyone who has shared a cell with you is five grand.'

I thank Derek and assure him I haven't discussed my case or anything of importance with Terry and never would.

When I return to my cell, I find Terry looking shamefaced. He confirms that he has spoken to the *Sun*, and they're keen to know when I'm being moved to Ford.

'You'll be on the front page tomorrow,' I warn him.

'No, no, I didn't tell them anything,' he insists.

I try not to laugh as I settle down to read through another three hundred letters that have been opened by the censor and left on the end of my bed. I can't believe he's had the time to read many, if any, of them.

When I've finished the last one, I lie back on my bed and reluctantly pick up Billy Little's twelve-page essay. I turn the first page. I cannot believe what I'm reading. He has such command of language, insight, and that rare gift of making the mundane interesting that I finish every word, before switching off the light a few minutes after ten. I have a feeling that you're going to hear a lot more about this man, and not just from me.

DAY 9   FRIDAY 27 JULY 2001

2.11 am

I am woken in the middle of the night by rap music blasting out from a cell on the other side of the block. I can't imagine what it must be like if you're trying to sleep in the next cell, or even worse in the bunk below. I'm told that rap music is the biggest single cause of fights breaking out in prison. I'm not surprised. I had to wait until it was turned off before I could get back to sleep. I didn't wake again until eight minutes past six. Amazingly, Terry can sleep through anything.

6.08 am

I write for two hours, and as soon as I've completed the first draft of what happened yesterday, I strip down to my underpants, put a towel round my waist, and place another one on the end of the bed with a bar of soap and a bottle of shampoo next to it.

My cell door is opened at eight twenty-three. I'm out of the starting gate like a thoroughbred, sprint along the corridor and into the shower room. Three of the four showers are already occupied by faster men than I. However, I still manage to capture the fourth stall, and once I've taken a long press-button shower, I feel clean for the first time in days.

When I return to my cell, Terry is still fast asleep, and even a prison officer unlocking the door doesn't disturb him. The new officer introduces himself as Ray Marcus, and explains that he works in the censor's department and is the other half of June Stelfox, who took care of my correspondence on House Block Three. His job is to check every item of mail a prisoner is sent, to make sure that they're not receiving anything that is against the regulations: razor blades, drugs, money – or even food. To be fair, although the censors open every letter, they don't read them. Ray is carrying a registered package which he slits open in front of me, and extracts a Bible. The eleventh in nine days. Like the others, I donate it to the chapel. He then asks if he can help in any way with my mail problem. Ray, as he prefers to be called, is courteous and seems almost embarrassed by the fact that I'm not allowed to open my own post. I tell him not to worry, because I haven't opened my own post for years.

I hand over three large brown envelopes containing all the letters I've received the day before, plus the first week (70 pages) of my handwritten script, together with twelve first-class stamps. I ask if they can all be sent back to my PA, Alison, so that she can carry on as if I was on holiday or abroad. He readily agrees, but points out that as senior censor, he is entitled to read anything that I am sending out.

'That's fine by me,' I tell him.

'I'd rather wait until it's published,' he says with a grin. 'After all, I've read everything else you've written.'

When he leaves he doesn't close my door, as if he knows what a difference this simple gesture makes to a man who will be locked up for twenty-two hours every day. This privilege lasts only for a few minutes before another officer strolling by slams it shut, but I am grateful nevertheless.

9.00 am

Breakfast. A bowl of cornflakes with UHT milk from a carton that has been open, and not seen a fridge, for the past twenty-four hours. Wonderful.

10.09 am

Another officer arrives to announce that the Chaplain would like to see me. Glorious escape. He escorts me to the chapel – no search this time – where David Powe is waiting for me. He is wearing the same pale beige jacket, grey flannel trousers and probably the same dog collar as he did when he conducted the service on Sunday. He is literally down at heel. We chat about how I'm settling in – doesn't everyone? – and then go on to discuss the fact that his sermon on Cain and Abel made it into *Private Eye*. He chuckles, obviously enjoying the notoriety.

David then talks about his wife, who's the headmistress of a local primary school, and has written two books for Harper-Collins on religion. They have two children, one aged thirteen and the other sixteen. When he talks about his parish – the other prisoners – it doesn't take me long to realize that he's a deeply committed Christian, despite his doubting and doubtful flock of murderers, rapists and drug addicts. However, he is delighted to hear that my cell-mate Terry reads the Bible every day. I confess to having never read Hebrews.

David asks me about my own religious commitment and I tell him that when I was the Conservative candidate for Mayor of London, I became aware of how many religions were being practised in the capital, and if there was a God, he had a lot of disparate groups representing him on Earth. He points out that in Belmarsh there are over a hundred Muslims, another hundred Roman Catholics, but that the majority of inmates are still C of E.

'What about the Jews?' I ask him.

'Only one or two that I know of,' he replies. 'Their family upbringing and sense of community is so strong that they rarely end up in the courts or prison.'

When the hour is up – everything seems to have an allocated time – he blesses me, and tells me that he hopes to see me back in church on Sunday.

As it's the biggest cell in the prison, he most certainly will.

11.10 am

Mr Weedon is waiting at the chapel door – sorry, barred gate – to escort me back to my cell. He says that Mr Marsland wants to see me again. Does this mean that they know when I'll be leaving Belmarsh and where I'll be going? I ask Mr Weedon but receive no response. When I arrive at Mr Marsland's office, Mr Loughnane and Mr Gates are also present. They all look grim. My heart sinks and I now understand why Mr Weedon felt unable to answer my question.

Mr Marsland says that Ford Open Prison have turned down my application because they feel they can't handle the press interest, so the whole matter has been moved to a higher level. For a moment I wonder if I will ever get out of this hellhole. He adds, hoping it will act as a sweetener, that he plans to move me into a single cell because Fossett (Terry) was caught phoning the *Sun*.

'I can see that you're disappointed about Ford,' he adds, 'but

DAY 9

we'll let you know where you'll be going, and when, just as soon as they tell us.' I get up to leave.

'I wonder if you'd be willing to give another talk on creative writing?' asks Mr Marsland. 'After your last effort, several other prisoners have told us that they want to hear you speak.'

'Why don't I just do an eight-week course,' I reply, 'as it seems we're going to be stuck with each other for the foreseeable future?' I immediately feel guilty about my sarcasm. After all, it isn't their fault that the Governor of Ford hasn't got the guts to try and handle a tricky problem. Perhaps he or she should read the Human Rights Act, and learn that this is not a fair reason to turn down my request.

2.00 pm

A woman officer unlocks the cell door, a cigarette hanging from her mouth,* and tells Terry he has a visitor. Terry can't believe it and tries to think who it could be. His father rarely speaks to him, his mother is dead, his brother is dying of Aids, he's lost touch with his sister and his cousin's in jail for murder. He climbs down from the top bunk, smiles for the first time in days, and happily troops out into the corridor, while I'm locked back in. I take advantage of Terry's absence and begin writing the second draft of yesterday's diary.

3.07 pm

Terry returns to the cell an hour later, dejected. A mistake must have been made because there turned out to be no visitor. They

---

* The Director General of Prisons, Martin Narey, has since issued a directive that officers should not smoke when on duty.

left him in the waiting room for over an hour while the other prisoners enjoyed the company of their family or friends.

I sometimes forget how lucky I am.

4.00 pm

Association. As I leave my cell and walk along the top landing, Derek Jones, a young double-strike prisoner, says he wants to show me something, and invites me back to his cell. He is one of those inmates whose tariff is open-ended, and although his case comes up for review by the Parole Board in 2005, he isn't confident that they will release him.

'I hear you're writing a book,' he says. 'But are you interested in things they don't know about out there?' he asks, staring through his barred window. I nod. 'Then I'll tell you something they don't even know about in here.' He points to a large stereo in the corner of the room – probably the one that kept me awake last night. It resembles a spaceship. 'That's my most valuable possession in the world,' he says. I don't interrupt. 'But I've got a problem.' I still say nothing. 'It runs on batteries, 'cause I haven't got any ice.'

'Ice? Why would you need ice for a ghetto blaster?'

'In Cell Electricity,' he says laughing.

'Ah, I see.'

'Have you any idea how much batteries cost?'

'No,' I tell him.

'£6.40 a time, and then they're only good for twelve hours, so I wouldn't be able to afford any tobacco if I had to buy new batteries every week.' I still haven't worked out where all this is leading. 'But I never have to buy any batteries, do I?'

'Don't you?' I say.

'No,' he replies, and then goes to a shelf behind his bed, and extracts a biro. He flicks off the little cap on the bottom and pulls out the refill, which has a coil of thin wire wrapped around it. He continues. 'First, I make an earth by scraping off a little paint from the water pipe behind my bed, then I take off the plastic cover from the strip light on the ceiling and attach the other end of the wire to the little box inside the light.' Derek can tell that I'm just about following this cunning subterfuge, when he adds, 'Don't worry about the details, Jeff, I've drawn you a diagram. [See page 105.] That way,' he says, 'I get an uninterrupted supply of electricity at Her Majesty's expense.'

My immediate reaction is, why isn't he on the outside doing a proper job? I thank him and assure Derek the story will get a mention in my story.

'What do I get out of it?' he asks. 'Because when I leave this place, all I have to my name other than that stereo is the ninety quid discharge money they give you.'*

I assure Derek that my publishers will pay him a fee for the use of the diagram if it appears in the book. We shake on it.

5.05 pm

Mr Weedon returns to tell me that I am being moved to a single cell. Terry immediately becomes petulant and starts shouting that he'd been promised a single cell even before I'd arrived.

'And you would have got one, Fossett,' Mr Weedon replies, 'if you hadn't phoned the press and grassed on your cell-mate for a few quid.'

Terry continues to harangue the officer and I can only

---

* Inmates are given £90 when leaving prison if they are of NFA (no fixed abode), £45 if they have somewhere to live. They can go back on social security after a fortnight.

1) ADD PAPER CLIP TO WIRE THAT LEADS FROM STEREO TO INNER BROWN. POWER INLET

2) USE INNER PEN TO ATTACH WIRE TO ⌐⌐⌐⌐ INLET

3) ALWAYS ATTACH WIRE TO PIPE FIRST

4) ALWAYS MAKE SURE WIRE (2) DOESN'T TOUCH. ANY OTHER METAL OR OTHER WIRE.

5) MAKE SURE WIRE (3) DOESN'T TOUCH ANYTHING METAL OTHER THAN PIPE.

6) MAKE SURE WIRE (3) TOUCHES BARE METAL ON PIPE. (CLEAR PAINT.)

7) USE OUTER PEN TO INSERT INTO WHERE PLACE POWER LEAD.

TO CELL PIPE

TO LIGHT

STEREO

Power Socket on Stereo

LIGHT →

CELL PIPE

wonder how long he will last with such a short fuse once he returns to the outside world.

I gather up my possessions and move across from Cell 40 to 30 on the other side of the corridor. My fourth move in nine days. A six-foot four-inch Ghanaian who was convicted of murdering a man in Peckham despite claiming that he was in Brighton with his girlfriend at the time, returns to his old bunk in Cell 40. I feel bad about depriving him of his private cell, and it becomes yet another reason I want to move to a D-cat prison as soon as possible, so that he can have his single cell back.

I spend an hour filling up my cellophane bag, carrying it across the corridor, emptying it, then rearranging my belongings in Cell 30. I have just completed this task when my new cell door is opened, and I'm ordered to go down to the hotplate for supper.

6.00 pm

I once again settle for the vegetarian option, although Paul (murder and stamps), who ticks off each name on a clipboard at the hotplate, tells me that the chicken is passable. I risk it. He's wrong again. I won't give him a third chance.

During Association I spend half an hour with Billy Little (murder) in his cell, going over his work. He tells me he has at least another twenty years to serve as his tariff is open-ended, so I advise him to start writing a novel, even a trilogy. He looks doubtful. He's not a man who's ever put much faith in the word of a Conservative.

There's a knock on the cell door and a massive giant of a man ambles into the room looking like a second-row forward in search of a scrum. I noticed him on the first day as he stood alone in the far corner of the room, staring silently through me.

He was hard to miss at over six foot, weighing around twenty-one stone. He's never said a word to me since my arrival on the spur, and I confess to being a little apprehensive about him, even frightened. He's known as Fletch.

He's come to 'let me know' that Terry is no longer complaining about my being moved into a single cell because he accepts that by phoning the *Sun* he was 'out of order', but he has since been warned that one of the Sunday papers is going to run a story about him hitting a woman over the head with a snooker ball wrapped in a sock. One of the many things prisoners will not tolerate is anyone attacking a woman. Terry has told Fletch that he's terrified that some of the inmates will beat him up once the story is published.* Fletch is letting it be known that he doesn't want any trouble, 'even though he accepts that the lad was stupid to have talked to the press in the first place'. Fletch looks at me and says, 'I must be the only person on the spur who hasn't spoken to you, but then I hate everything you stand for. Don't take it personally,' he adds and then leaves without another word.

Billy tells me that Fletch is one of the most respected prisoners on the spur and, to my surprise, a Listener. 'Don't worry about him,' he adds, 'because I can tell you that one of the reasons we have so little trouble on this wing is because he was a bouncer for a London nightclub before he ended up in here. Last year he single-handedly stopped a riot over the state of the food. The screws could never have contained the problem on their own, and they know it.'

---

* Beatings up (hammerings) usually take place in the shower room, which is why some prisoners don't wash from one year to the next. The reason the shower room is the preferred place for retribution is because it's on the top floor at the end of a long corridor, more than four prisoners are allowed to congregate at any one time, and any excess noise is usually ignored as exuberance.

DAY 9

I leave Billy and return to Association to play a couple of hands of Kaluki with Del Boy (murder), Colin (GBH) and Paul (murder – seventy-five years between them). I win the first hand and lose the second by 124 points. It's been that sort of a day.

Just as I'm about to return to my cell for lock-up, Ms Roberts appears on the floor. Terry rushes across to her and begins an animated conversation. She does her best to calm him down. When he is placated enough to move on, I ask her if she's had a call from my solicitor.

'Yes,' she replies, 'and I'll have a word with you first thing in the morning. I hope you'll feel it's good news.' I don't press her for any details because several other prisoners have formed a queue as they also wish to speak to the Deputy Governor before lock-up.

9.00 pm

It has, as I have already stated, been an up and down sort of day, but I feel a little better after Ms Roberts' comments. What will she have to tell me tomorrow?

For the next couple of hours I go through another hundred letters that the censor has left on my bed. The pattern is now firmly set, but there is one letter in particular that amuses me – *I am writing to give you my full support, as I suspect that no one else is bothering to do so at the present time.* I smile because Ms Buxton of Northants reminds me just how fortunate I am to have so many people willing to fight my corner. I only have to think about Terry's phantom visitor to realize just how lucky I am.

DAY 10   SATURDAY 28 JULY 2001

5.42 am

I wake in a cold sweat, having had the strangest dream. I'm back at Oxford in the sixties, where I win the University cross-country trials, which would automatically ensure that I was awarded a Blue and a place in the team against Cambridge. As I ran the one hundred yards in my youth, this scenario seems somewhat unlikely. But it gets worse. I'm disqualified, and the race is awarded to the man who came second. When the cup is presented to him I lose my temper with the judges. The judges are David Coleman and the late Ron Pickering – two of the most decent men God ever put on Earth. They tell me they had to disqualify me because they just didn't believe I could possibly have won. No doubt the prison psychiatrist will have a theory.

6.11 am

I don't begin writing immediately as I consider the task I have set myself over the past few days: a close study of lifers.

DAY 10

On spur one, there are fifty-two men serving life sentences.* I've now held long conversations with about twenty of them, and have come to the conclusion that they fall roughly into two categories. This is of course an over-simplification, as each individual is both complex and unique. The first group consist of those who insist, 'It wasn't me, guv, it was all a stitch up. They didn't even find the murder weapon, but because of my previous record I fitted neatly into the required police profile.'

The other group hold their hands in the air and admit to a moment of madness, which they will eternally regret, and accept they must pay the penalty the law demands. One or two even add, 'It's no more than I deserve.'

My natural sense of justice makes me worry about the first group; are they all liars, or is there anyone on this spur serving a life sentence who is in fact innocent? But more of that later.

9.00 am

Saturdays differ from every other day of the week because you're not supplied with a plastic bag containing breakfast the night before when you queue for supper. At 9 am your cell door is opened and you go down to the canteen for a cooked breakfast – egg, beans and chips. I accept the egg and beans, and wonder how many Saturdays it will be before I'm willing to add the chips.

---

* On 30 June 1990, there were 1,725 inmates serving life sentences. On 30 June 2000 this figure had risen by 163 per cent to 4,540, 97 per cent of them male, of whom 3,405 were convicted murderers. It's important to remember that murderers are different to other criminals. For over 50 per cent it's a first offence, and when they are released, they never commit another crime. It's equally true to say that the other 50 per cent are professional criminals, who do not deserve a moment of your sympathy.

10.00 am

I'm given the choice of taking exercise in the yard, or remaining banged-up in my cell. I sign up for exercise.

On the first two circuits of the yard I'm joined by a group of drug dealers who ask me if I need anything, from marijuana to crack cocaine to heroin. It takes them some time to accept that I've never taken a drug in my life, and don't intend to start now.

'We do a lot of business with your lot,' one of them adds casually.

I would like to have replied, 'And I hope you rot in jail for the rest of your life,' but didn't have the guts.

The next inmate to join me is a hot-gospeller who hopes that while I'm in Belmarsh I'll discover Christ. I explain that I consider one's religion to be a personal and private matter, but thank him for his concern. He isn't quite that easy to shake off and sticks with me for five more circuits: unlike a visit from a Jehovah's Witness, there's no way of slamming the front door.

I hope to manage a few circuits on my own so I can think for a moment, but no such luck because I'm joined by a couple of East End tearaways who want my opinion on their upcoming court case. I warn them that my knowledge of the law is fairly sketchy, so perhaps I'm the wrong person to approach. One of them becomes abusive, and for the first time since arriving at Belmarsh, I'm frightened and fearful for my own safety. Paul has already warned me that there might well be the odd prisoner who would stick a knife in me just to get himself on the front pages and impress his girlfriend.

Within moments, Billy Little and Fletch are strolling a pace behind me, obviously having sensed the possible danger, and although the two young hooligans are not from our spur, one look at Fletch and they are unlikely to try anything. The tear-aways peel off, but I have a feeling they will hang around and bide their time. Perhaps it would be wise for me to avoid the exercise yard for a couple of days.

I'm finally joined by a charming young black prisoner, who wants to tell me about his drumming problem. It takes another couple of circuits before I realize that he doesn't play in a rock band; drumming is simply slang for burglary. I consider this particular experience a bit of a watershed. If you didn't know what 'drumming' was before you began reading this diary, you're probably as naive as I am. If you did, these scribblings may well be commonplace.

12 noon

Lunch. I am now a fully fledged vegetarian. Outside of prison I founded a club known as VAF and VOP, which many of my friends have become members of after sending a donation to the Brompton Hospital.* VAF is 'vegetarian at functions'. I have long believed that it is impossible, even in the best-run establishments, to prepare three hundred steaks as each customer would wish them cooked, so I always order the vegetarian alternative because I know it will have been individually prepared. VOP stands for 'vegetarian on planes'. I suspect many of you are already members of this club, and if you are, pay up and send your five pounds to the Brompton Hospital immediately. I am now adding VIP to my list, and can only hope that none of you ever qualify for membership.

---

*I am an admirer of the eminent heart surgeon, Sir Magdi Yacoub, and any donation you give will assist his current research.

2.00 pm

The cell door is opened and I am told that Ms Roberts wants to see me. I feel my heart pounding as I try to recall her exact words the previous evening.

When I join her in a room just off the bubble, she immediately confirms that my solicitors have been in touch, and she has told them that she wants me out of Belmarsh as quickly as possible. She adds that they moved Barry George (murder of Jill Dando) this morning, and I'm due out next. However, she has just received a phone call from a chief inspector in the Metropolitan Police, to warn her that they have received a letter from the Baroness Emma Nicholson, demanding an inquiry into what happened to the £57 million I raised for the Kurds.

I assure Ms Roberts that I was in no way involved with the receiving or distribution of any monies for the Kurds, as that was entirely the responsibility of the Red Cross. She nods.

'If the police confirm that they will not be following up Ms Nicholson's inquiry, then we should have you out of Belmarsh and off to a D-cat by the end of the week.'

As I have always in the past believed in justice, I assume that the police will quickly confirm that I was not involved in any way.

Ms Roberts goes on to confirm that Ford, my first choice, is unwilling to take me because of the publicity problem, but she hopes to discuss some alternatives with me on Monday.

Ms Roberts suggests that as my next lecture is coming up on Thursday, I should be released from my cell from nine in the morning until five in the afternoon, so I can prepare for the talk in the library where I will have access to reference books. She knows only too well that I can give this talk without a moment's preparation but, unlike the Baroness Nicholson, she is concerned about what I'm going through.

4.00 pm

Association. During the Saturday afternoon break, I go down to the ground floor, hoping to watch some cricket on the TV, but I have to settle for horse racing as a large number of prisoners are already sitting round the set intent on following the King George VI and Queen Elizabeth Stakes at Ascot. The sport of kings has never been one of those pastimes that I've taken a great deal of interest in. I've long accepted George Bernard Shaw's maxim on horse racing, that *it's nothing more than a plot between the upper classes and the lower classes to fleece the middle classes*. I turn away from the television and see a slight, rather anaemic-looking young man standing alone in the corner. He's wearing a raspberry-coloured tracksuit, the official garb of prisoners who do not have their own clothes. I've not come across him before, but he looks a most unlikely murderer. I stroll across to join Fletch, who I feel confident will know exactly who he is.

'He's got twenty-one days for shoplifting,' Fletch tells me, 'and has a mental age of about eleven.' He pauses. 'They should never have sent him to Belmarsh in the first place.'

'Then why put him on the lifers' wing?' I ask.

'For his own protection,' says Fletch. 'He was attacked in the yard during exercise this afternoon, and some other cons continued to bully him when he returned to Block Two. He's only got nine more days left to serve so they've put him in my cell.' Now I understand why there are two beds in Fletch's cell, as I suspect this is not an unusual solution for someone in distress.

One of the phones becomes free – a rare occurrence – so I take advantage of it and call Mary in Grantchester. She's full of news, including the fact that the former head of the prison service, Sir David Ramsbotham, has written to *The Times* saying it was inappropriate to send me to prison – community service would have been far more worthwhile. She tells me she also has a sackful of letters talking about the iniquity of the judge's summing-up – not to mention the sentence – and she's beginning to wonder if there might be the possibility of a retrial. I think not. Mr Justice Potts has retired, and the last thing the establishment would want to do is embarrass him.

After thirty-seven years of marriage I know Mary so well that I can hear the strain of the last few weeks in her voice. I recall Ms Roberts' words the first time we met: 'It can be just as traumatic for your immediate family on the outside, as it is for you on the inside.' My two-pound BT phonecard is about to run out, but not before I tell her that she's a veritable Portia and I am no Brutus.

The moment I put the phone down, I find another lifer, Colin (GBH), standing by my side. He wants to have a word about his application to do an external degree at Ruskin College, Oxford. I have already had several chats with Colin, and he makes an interesting case study. In his youth (he's now thirty-five), he was a complete wastrel and tearaway, which included a period of being a professional football hooligan. In fact, he has written a fascinating piece on the subject, in which he now admits that he is ashamed of what he got up to. Colin has been in and out of jail for most of his adult life, and even when he's inside, he feels it is nothing less than his duty to take the occasional swing at a prison officer. This always ends with a spell in segregation and time being added to his sentence. On one occasion he even lost a couple of teeth, which you can't miss whenever he grins.

'That's history,' he tells me, because he now has a purpose. He wants to leave prison with a degree, and qualifications that will ensure he gets a real job. There is no doubt about his ability. Colin is articulate and bright, and having read his essays and literary criticism, I have no doubt that if he wants to sit for a degree, it's well within his grasp. And this is a man who couldn't read or write before he entered prison. I have a real go at him, assuring him that he's clever enough to take a degree and to get on with it. I start pummelling him on the chest as if he was a punch bag. He beams over to the duty officer seated behind the desk at the far end of the room.

'Mr King, this prisoner is bullying me,' says Colin, in a plaintive voice.

The officer smiles. 'What have you been saying to him, Archer?'

I repeat the conversation word for word.

'Quite agree with you, Archer,' he says, and returns to reading the *Sun*.

6.00 pm

Supper. Vegetarian fingers, overcooked and greasy, peas that are glued together, and a plastic mug of Highland Spring (49p).

8.00 pm

I've just finished checking over my script for the day when my cell door is opened by an officer. Fletch is standing in the doorway and asks if he can join me for a moment, which I welcome. He takes a seat on the end of the bed, and I offer him a mug of blackcurrant juice. Fletch reminds me that he's a Listener, and adds that he's there if I need him.

He then begins to explain the role of Listeners and how they came into existence after a fifteen-year-old boy hanged himself in a Cardiff jail some ten years ago. He passes me a single sheet of paper that explains their guidelines. (See page 117.) Among

The Listeners

Who are they?
How do I contact them?
How do I know I can trust them?

Listeners are inmates, just as you are, who have been trained by the **Samaritans** in both suicide awareness and befriending skills.

You can talk to a Listener about anything in complete confidence, just as you would a Samaritan. **Everything you say is treated with confidentiality.**

Listeners are rarely shocked and **you don't have to be suicidal** to talk to one. If you have any worries or concerns, however great or small, **they are there for you.** If you have concerns about a friend or cellmate and feel unable to approach a member of the spur staff or healthcare team, then please tell a Listener in confidence. **It is not grassing and it may save a life.**

Listeners are easy to contact. Their names are displayed on orange cards on their cell doors and on most notice boards throughout the House-Blocks or ask any member of the spur staff.

Listeners are all bound by a code of **confidentiality** that doesn't only run from House-Block to House-Block but also through a great number of Prisons throughout the country. Any breach of that confidentiality would cause irreparable damage to the benefits achieved, and because of this code Listeners are now as firmly established as your cell door.

Fletch's responsibilities is to spot potential bullies and – perhaps more important – potential victims, as most victims are too frightened to give you a name because they fear revenge at a later date, either inside or outside of prison.

I ask him to share some examples with me. He tells me that there are two heroin addicts on the spur and although he won't name them, it's hard not to notice that a couple of the younger lifers on the ground floor have needle tracks up and down their arms. One of them is only nineteen and has tried to take his own life twice, first with an overdose, and then later when he attempted to cut his wrist with a razor.

'We got there just in time,' says Fletch. 'After that, the boy was billeted with me for five weeks.'

Fletch feels it's also vitally important to have a good working relationship with the prison staff – he doesn't call them screws or kangaroos – otherwise the system just can't work. He admits there will always be an impenetrable barrier, which he describes as the iron door, but he has done his best to break this down by forming a prison committee of three inmates and three officers who meet once a month to discuss each other's problems. He says with some considerable pride that there hasn't been a serious incident on *his* spur for the past eight months.

He then tells me a story about an occasion when he was released from prison some years ago for a previous offence. He decided to call into his bank and cash a cheque. He climbed the steps, stood outside the bank and waited for someone to open the door for him. He looks up from the end of the bed at the closed cell door. 'You see, it doesn't have a handle on our side, so you always have to wait for someone to open it. After so long in prison, I'd simply forgotten how to open a door.'

Fletch goes on to tell me that being a Listener gives him a

reason for getting up each day. But like all of us, he has his own problems. He's thirty-seven, and will be my age, sixty-one, when he is eventually released.

'The truth is that I'll never see the outside world again.' He pauses. 'I'll die in prison.' He pauses again. 'I just haven't decided when.'

Fletch has unwittingly made me his Listener.

DAY 11   SUNDAY 29 JULY 2001

6.27 am

Sundays are not a good day in prison because you spend so much time locked up in your cell. When you ask why, the officers simply say, 'It's because we're short-staffed.' I can at least use six of those hours writing.

Many of the lifers have long-term projects, some of which I have already mentioned. One is writing a book, another taking a degree, a third is a dedicated Listener. In fact, although I may have to spend most of today locked up in my cell, Fletch, Billy, Tony, Paul, Andy and Del Boy all have responsible jobs which allow them to roam around the block virtually unrestricted. This makes sense, because if a prisoner has a long sentence, they may feel they have nothing to lose by causing trouble, but once you've given them privileges – and not being locked up all day is unquestionably a privilege – they're unlikely to want to give up that freedom easily.

8.03 am

I shave using a Bic razor supplied by HMP. They give you a new razor every day, and it is a punishable offence to be found with two of them in your cell, so every evening, just before lock-up, you trade in your old one for a new one.

As soon as the cell door is opened, I make a dash for the shower, but four young West Indians get there before me. One of them, Dennis (GBH), has the largest bag of toiletries I have ever seen. It's filled with several types of deodorant and after-shave lotions. He is a tall, well-built, good-looking guy who rarely misses a gym session. When I tease him about the contents of his bag, Dennis simply replies, 'You've got to be locked up for a long time, Jeff, before you can build up such a collection on twelve-fifty a week.' Another of them eventually emerges from his shower stall and comments about my not having flipflops on my feet. 'Quickest way to get verrucas,' he warns me. 'Make sure Mary sends you in a pair as quickly as possible.'

Having repeatedly to push the button with the palm of one hand while you soap yourself with the other is a new skill I have nearly mastered. However, when it comes to washing your hair, you suddenly need three hands. I wish I were an octopus.

When I'm finally dry, my three small thin green prison towels are all soaking – I should only have one, but thanks to Del Boy ... I return to my cell, and because I'm so clean, I'm made painfully aware of the prison smell. If you've ever travelled on a train for twenty hours and then slept in a station waiting room for the next eight, you're halfway there. Once I've put back on yesterday's clothes, I pour myself another bowl of cornflakes. I think I can make the packet (£1.47) last for seven helpings before I'll need to order another one. I hear my name being bellowed out by an officer on the ground floor, but decide to finish my cornflakes before reporting to him – first signs of rebellion?

When I do report, Mr Bentley tells me that there's a parcel for me in reception. This time no one escorts me on the journey, or bothers to search me when I arrive. The parcel turns out to be a plastic bag full of clothes sent in by Mary: two shirts, five T-shirts, seven pairs of pants, seven pairs of socks, two pairs of gym shorts, a tracksuit, and two sweaters. The precise allocation that prison regulations permit. Once back in my cell I discard my two-day-old pants and socks to put on a fresh set of clothes, and now not only feel clean, but almost human.

I spend a considerable time arranging the rest of my clothes in the little cupboard above my bed and as it has no shelves this becomes something of a challenge. (See pages 124–125.)* Once I've completed the exercise, I sit on the end of the bed and wait to be called for church.

10.39 am

My name is among several others bellowed out by the officer at the front desk on the ground floor, followed by the single word 'church'. All those wishing to attend the service report to the middle landing and wait by the barred gate near the bubble. Waiting in prison for your next activity is not unlike hanging around for the next bus. It might come along in a few moments, or you may have to wait for half an hour. Usually the latter.

While I'm standing there, Fletch joins me on the second-floor landing to warn me that there's an article in the *News of the World* suggesting that I'm 'lording it' over the other prisoners. Apparently I roam around in the unrestricted areas in a white shirt, watching TV, while all the other prisoners are locked up. He says that although everyone on the spur knows it's a joke, the rest of the block (three other spurs) do not. Fletch advises

---

* This picture of my cell was drawn by Derek Jones. I was not allowed to take a photograph of it.

me to avoid the exercise yard today, as someone might want 'to make something of it'.

The more attentive readers will recall that my white shirt was taken away from me last week because I could be mistaken for an officer; my feeble attempt to watch cricket on TV ended in having to follow the progress of the King George VI and Queen Elizabeth Stakes; and by now all of you know how many hours I've been locked in my cell. How the *News of the World* can get every fact wrong surprises even me.

The heavy, barred gate on the middle floor is eventually opened, and I join prisoners from the other three spurs who wish to attend the morning service. Although everyone is searched, they now hardly bother with me. The process has become not unlike going through a customs check at Heathrow. There are two searchers on duty this morning, one male and one female officer. I notice the queue to be searched by the woman is longer than the one for the man. One of the lifers whispers, 'They can't add anything to your sentence for what you're thinking.'

When I enter the chapel I return to my place in the second row. This time the congregation is almost 80 per cent black, despite the population of the prison being around fifty–fifty. The service is conducted by a white officer from the Salvation Army, and his small band of singers are also all white. When I next see Mr Powe, I must remember to tell him how many churches, not so far away from Belmarsh, have magnificent black choirs and amazing preachers who encourage you to cry Alleluia. Something else I learnt when I was candidate for Mayor.

This week I notice that the congregation is roughly split in two, with a sort of demarcation zone about halfway back. The prisoners seated in the first eight rows have only one purpose – to follow every line in the Bible that the Chaplain refers to, to sing at the top of their voices and participate fully in the spirit of

the service. The back nine rows show scant interest in proceedings, and I observe that they have formed smaller groups of two, three or four, their heads bowed deep in conversation. I assume they're friends from different spurs and find the service one of the few opportunities to meet up, chat, and pass on messages. Quite possibly even drugs – if they are willing to go through a fairly humiliating process.*

The Chaplain's text this Sunday comes from the Gospel of St John, and concentrates in particular on the prodigal son. Last week it was Cain and Abel. I can only assume that next week it will be Honour Among Thieves.

The Chaplain tells his flock that he is only going to speak to them for five minutes, and then addresses us for twelve, but to be fair, he was quite regularly interrupted with cries of 'Alleluia', and 'Bless us, Lord'. The Chaplain's theme is that if you leave the bosom of your family, try to make it alone, and things go wrong, it doesn't mean that your father won't welcome you back if you are willing to admit you've made mistakes. Many of those in the front four rows start jumping up and down and cheering.

After the service is over, and we have all been searched again, I'm escorted back to House Block One, but not before several inmates from Block Three come across to say hello. Remember Mark, Kevin and Dave? I'm brought up to date with all of their hopes and expectations as we slowly make our way back to our separate blocks. No one moves quickly in prison, because it's just another excuse to spend more time out of your cell. As I pass the desk at the end of my spur, I spot a pile of Sunday newspapers. The *News of the World* is by far the most

---

* Drugs are often packed into a condom and then pushed up the rectum. Transferring them in the back pew of the chapel can't be a pleasant experience.

popular, followed by the *Sunday Mirror*, but there is also quite a large order for the *Sunday Times*.

When I return to my cell, I find my room has been swept and tidied, and my bed made up with clean sheets. I'm puzzled, because there was nothing in the prison handbook about room service. I find out later that the Ghanaian murderer wants to thank me for helping him write a letter to his mother. Returning favours is far more commonplace in prison than it is outside.

12 noon

Lunch: grated cheese, a tomato, a green apple and a mug of Highland Spring. I'm running out of water and will in future have to order more bottles of Highland Spring and less chocolate from the canteen.

After lunch I sit down to write the second draft of this morning's script, as I won't be let out again until four, and then only for sixty minutes. I clean my glasses and notice that without thinking, I've begun to split my double Kleenex tissue so that I can make the maximum use of both sheets.

4.00 pm

Association. During the hour break, I don't join the others in the yard for exercise because of the *News of the World* article, which means I'll be stuck inside all day. I can't remember the last time I remained indoors for twenty-four hours.

I join Fletch (murder) in his cell, along with Billy (murder) and Tony (marijuana only, escaped to Paris). They're discussing in great detail an article in the *Sunday Times* about paedophiles, and I find myself listening intently. Because on this subject, as in many others concerning what goes on in prison, I recall Lord

Longford's words, 'Don't assume all prisoners have fixed views.' I feel on safer ground when the discussion turns to the Tory Party leadership. Only Tony, who reads *The Times*, can be described as a committed liberalist. Most of the others, if they are anything, are New Labour.*

They all agree that Ken Clarke is a decent enough sort of bloke – pint at the local and all that, and not interested in his appearance, but they know very little about Iain Duncan Smith, other than he comes from the right wing of the Party and therefore has to be their enemy. I suggest that it's never quite that simple. IDS has clear views on most issues, and they shouldn't just label him in that clichéd way. He's a complex and thoughtful man – his father, I remind them, was a Second World War hero, flying Spitfires against the Germans and winning the DSO and Bar. They like that. I suspect if we were at war now, his son would be doing exactly the same thing.

'But he has the same instincts as Ann Widdecombe,' says Fletch. 'Bang 'em up and throw away the key.'

'That may well be the case, but don't forget Ann is supporting Ken Clarke, despite his views on Europe.'

'That doesn't add up,' says Billy.

'Politics is like prison,' I suggest. 'You mustn't assume anything, as the exact opposite often turns out to be the reality.'

5.00 pm

'Back to your cells,' bellows a voice.

I leave the lifers and return to my cell on the top floor to be incarcerated, supper excepted, until nine tomorrow morning –

---

* Convicted prisoners, Members of the House of Lords, and certified lunatics are ineligible to vote. I now qualify in two of the three categories.

sixteen hours. Think about it, sixteen hours. That's the length of time you will spend between rising in the morning and going to bed at night.

Just as I arrive at my door, another lifer (Doug) hands me an envelope. 'It's from a prisoner on Block Two,' he says. 'He evidently told you all about it yesterday when you were in the exercise yard.' I throw the envelope on the bed and switch on the radio, to be reminded that it's the hottest day of the year (92°). I open my little window to its furthest extent (six inches) to let in whatever breeze there is, but I still feel myself sweating as I sit at my desk checking over the day's script. I glance up at the cupboard behind my bed, grateful for the clean clothes that Mary sent in this morning.

6.00 pm

Supper. I can't face the hotplate, despite Tony's recommendation of Spam fritter, so I have another portion of grated cheese, open a small tin of coleslaw (41p) and – disaster – finish the last drop of my last bottle of Highland Spring. Thank heavens that it's canteen tomorrow and I'm allowed to spend another £12.50.

During the early evening, I go over my manuscript, and as there are no letters to deal with, I turn my attention to the envelope that was handed to Doug in the yard. It turns out to be a TV script for a thirty-minute pilot set in a women's prison. It's somehow been smuggled out of Holloway and into Belmarsh (no wonder it's easy to get hold of drugs). The writer has a good ear for prison language, and allows you an interesting insight into life in a women's prison, but I fear *Cell Block H* and *Bad Girls* have already done this theme to death. It's fascinating to spot the immediate differences in a women's prison to Belmarsh. Not least the searching procedure, the fact that lesbianism is far more

prevalent in female prisons than homosexuality is in male establishments, and, if you can believe it, the level of violence is higher.
They don't bother waiting until you're in the shower before they
throw the first punch. Anywhere, at any time, will do.

It's a long hot evening, and I have visits from Del Boy, Paul,
Fletch and finally Tony.

Tony (hotplate, marijuana only, escaped to Paris) started life
as a B-cat prisoner, and was transferred after three and a half
years to Ford Open (first offence, no history of violence). After
eight blameless months they allowed him out on a town visit,
so he happily set off for Bognor Regis. But after four visits to
that seaside resort during the next four months, he became
somewhat bored with the cold, deserted beach and the limited
shopping centre. That's when he decided there were other towns
he'd like to visit on his day off.

When they let him out the following month, he took the
boat-train to Paris.

The prison authorities were not amused. It was only when
he moved on to Spain, two years later, that they finally caught
up with him and he was arrested. After spending sixteen months
in a Spanish jail waiting to be deported (canteen, fifty pounds a
week, and no bang-up until nine), they sent him back to the UK.
Tony now resides in this high-security double A-Category
prison, from where no one has ever escaped, and will remain put
until he has completed his full sentence (twelve years). No time
was added to his sentence, but there will be no remission (half
off for good behaviour) and he certainly won't be considered for
an open prison again. This fifty-four-year-old somehow keeps
smiling and even manages to tell his story with self-deprecating
humour.

Tony leaves me with a copy of the *Sunday Mirror*. Although
it's not a paper I'm in the habit of reading, I am at least able to

bring myself up to date on the county cricket scores, not to mention who among the fighting fit will find a place in the England team for the third Test against Australia on Thursday. My beloved Somerset are in second place in the county championship and doing well in their current fixture against Glamorgan. On the England front, the *Mirror*'s cricket correspondent is suggesting it's time to bring back Tufnell. I did an auction for Phil during his testimonial year, and although he's not always popular with the selectors, the packed banqueting hall at the Dorchester proved the regard in which he is held by the Middlesex supporters. It seems that Thorpe, Hussain, Vaughan and Croft are all injured and will not make the starting line while a reluctant Atherton will be called on once again to skipper the side. It doesn't seem to improve his batting.

Meanwhile, Australia fields the same team that so roundly defeated us at Lords. I always thought it was the visiting side that was meant to have injury problems.

I finally finish *The Moon's a Balloon*, which left me with the distinct feeling that Mr Niven must have lived a charmed life. I only met him once, and that was at a literary luncheon in Yorkshire, where he was on the circuit with *Bring on the Empty Horses*, the sequel to the book I've just finished reading. It was an occasion I shall never forget, because the other author was James Herriot of *It Shouldn't Happen to a Vet* fame. I was there to launch my first effort, *Not A Penny More, Not A Penny Less*, and was naturally delighted to be among such illustrious company. After the speeches had concluded, the authors were each escorted to a table, so that they could sign copies of their books.

Mr Niven's queue stretched across the dining-room floor and out of the front door, while Mr Herriot's fans were almost as legion. In my case, I didn't have a single customer. When the signing was over, Mr Niven graciously came across to my table, purchased a copy of *Penny*, and told me he would read it on the flight back to Los Angeles the following day. He turned out to be one of the three people who paid for the book. A generous gesture, which many people have since told me was typical. But imagine my surprise when a few days later I received a hand-written letter from the Bel Air Hotel.

> *Dear Jeffrey,*
> *Much enjoyed Penny, have no doubt it will sell even more*
> *copies than Horses by the time you're my age.*
> > *Yours ever*
> > *David*

10.00 pm

Bang on ten, the rap music begins blasting out.

> Gunshot to the head, pussyboy gets dead
> Gunshot to the head, pussyboy gets dead
> Gunshot to the head, pussyboy gets dead
> Gunshot to the head, pussyboy gets dead
> Gunshot to the head, pussyboy gets dead
> Gunshot to the head, pussyboy gets dead . . .

Have you ever stopped at a traffic light to find yourself next to an open car with its radio full on? Do you then allow the offending driver to accelerate away? Imagine being in a cell with the music blasting out on both sides of you, but you can't accelerate away.

DAY 12   MONDAY 30 JULY 2001

6.03 am

Overslept, but then woken by the Alsatians off on their morning rounds. They are every bit as reliable as an alarm clock, but not as cheerful or optimistic as a cockerel. I put on a tracksuit, sit down at my desk and write for two hours.

8.10 am

A bowl of cornflakes with UHT milk, plus the added luxury of a banana which Del Boy has smuggled out of the canteen. I sit on the end of the bed and wait to see what fate has in store for me.

10.00 am

I'm told I must report to the workshops, despite putting my name down for education. Another long trek to a different part of the building. This time we're escorted into a large square room about the same size as the chapel, but with whitewashed, unadorned brick walls. The first person I recognize is Fletch, who is seated next to a prison officer behind a trestle table at the top of the room. He's obviously the works manager.

The work room has five rows of tables, each about thirty feet in length, with prisoners seated on both sides making up a chain gang. My group consists of four inmates whose purpose is to fill a small plastic bag with all the ingredients necessary to make a cup of tea. In the centre of the table placed between us are large plastic buckets heaped with small packets. At the bottom end of the table sits a silent Serb, who places four sachets of sugar in each bag and then pushes his contribution across the table to a Lebanese man who adds three sachets of milk. He then passes the bag on to an inmate from Essex who drops in three teabags, before it's passed over to me. My job is to seal up the bag and drop it in the large open bucket at my end of the table.

Every fifteen minutes or so another prisoner, whose name I never discover, comes and empties the bucket. This mind-numbing exercise continues for approximately two hours, for which I will be credited with two pounds in my canteen account.

The Serb (sugar) who sits at the other end of the table is, I would guess, around thirty. He's unwilling to discuss anything except the fate of ex-President Milošević, and the fact that he isn't cooperating with the European Court in the Hague. He will not talk about his crime or the length of his sentence.

Ali, the Lebanese man (powdered milk) who sits opposite me, is more forthcoming. He's been found guilty of 'breach of trust'. Ali tells me that he worked for a well-known credit-card company, and after several years was promoted to manager of a London branch. During that time he became infatuated with an American lady, who could best be described as high-maintenance, and used to the sort of lifestyle he couldn't afford. Ali began to borrow (his words) money from the company safe each night. He would then take her to a casino, where they would have a free meal, before he began working the tables. If he won, he would put the money back in the safe the next morning. If he lost, he would borrow even more the following evening. One night he won £5,000 and returned every penny the following day.

By the time his girlfriend had dumped him and flown back to the States, Ali had 'borrowed' £28,000. He decided to come clean and report the whole incident to his boss, assuring the company that it was his intention to repay every penny.

Ali then sold his house, cashed in his life-insurance policy, pawned a few valuables and reimbursed the company in full. He was later arrested, charged with breach of trust, and last Friday sent down for eighteen months. He will probably end up serving seven months and is due to be transferred to Ford (D-cat) next week. He is fifty-three, an intelligent and articulate man, who accepts that he will never be able to work in this country again. He plans to go to America or return to the Lebanon, where he hopes to begin a new life.

My former secretary, Angie Peppiatt, the Crown's main witness in my case, admitted to the same offence – breach of trust – while giving evidence at my trial. In her case she wasn't able to explain how thousands of pounds went missing, other than to smile at the judge and say, 'I have done things I am ashamed of, but it was the culture of the time.' I have recently asked my solicitor to place the full details in the hands of the police and see if she is subject to the same rigorous inquiry as I was. You may well know the answer by the time this book is published.

The Essex man (teabags) sitting next to Ali boasts to anyone who cares to listen that he is a professional gangster who specializes in robbing banks. The gang consists of his brother-in-law, a friend and himself. He tells me they make a very profitable living, but expect to spend at least half of their working lives in jail. He and Ali could not be more different.

The prisoner who turns up every fifteen minutes to empty

the large bucket at the end of the table doesn't hang around, so I can't discover much about him, other than he's twenty-three, this is his first offence, his case hasn't come before the court yet, and he's hoping to get off. If he doesn't, he tells me, he'll use the time to study for an Open University history degree. I don't think he realizes that he's just admitted that he's guilty.

A hooter blasts to indicate that the one hundred and twenty minutes are finally up, we are all escorted back to our separate spurs, and lunch.

12 noon

Lunch. What's on offer is so bad that I have to settle for a small tin of Heinz potato salad (61p) and three McVitie's biscuits (17p). As I return from the hotplate I see Andy leaning up against the fence that divides the spur from the canteen area. He pushes a bottle of Highland Spring through a triangle of wire mesh – the high point of my day.

2.00 pm

The Chaplain, David Powe, makes an unscheduled visit to my cell. He's wearing his dog collar, the same beige coat, the same dark grey trousers, and the same shoes as he has at the previous meetings. I can only conclude that he must be paid even less than the prison officers. He's kept his promise and got hold of some drawing paper for Derek Jones, who can't afford more than one pad a week.

The Chaplain goes on to tell me that he and his family will be off on holiday for the next three weeks, and just in case he doesn't see me again, he would like to wish me luck with my appeal, and hopes I'll be sent in the near future to somewhere a little less foreboding than Belmarsh. Before he leaves, I read to him my description of the service he conducted last week. He chuckles at the Cain and Abel reference – a man able to laugh at himself. He leaves me a few moments later to go in search of Derek, and hand over the drawing pads.

It was some hours later that I felt racked with guilt by the thought he must have paid for the paper out of his own pocket.

2.48 pm

My door is unlocked by Ms Taylor who enters the cell carrying what looks like a tuning fork. She goes over to my window and taps the four bars one by one.

'Just want to make sure you haven't loosened them, or tried to replace them,' she explains. 'Wouldn't want you to escape, would we?'

I'm puzzled by Ms Taylor's words because it's a sheer drop of some seventy feet from the third floor down to the exercise yard, and then you would still have to climb over a thirty-five-foot wall, topped with razor wire, to escape. Houdini would have been stretched to consider such a feat. I later learn that there's another thirty-five foot wall beyond that, not to mention a few dozen Alsatians who don't respond to the command, 'Sit, Rover.'

I can only conclude it's in the prison manual under the heading, 'tasks to be carried out, once a day, once a week, once a year, once in a lifetime'.*

---

* I checked later. It *is* in the prison regulations, under 'Locks, Bolts and Bars'.

DAY 12

4.00 pm

I've put my name down for the gym again as I'm now desperate to get some exercise. When an officer hollers out, 'Gym,' I'm first in the queue that congregates on the middle floor. When the gate is opened, I'm informed by the duty Gym Instructor that only eight prisoners can participate from any one spur, and my name was the twelfth to be registered. The low point of my day.

I return to the ground floor and watch the first half of a Humphrey Bogart black-and-white movie, where Bogey is a sea dog who plays a major part in winning the war in the North Atlantic. However, we are all sent back to our cells at five, so I never discover if it was the Germans or the Americans who won the last War.

5.20 pm

I have an unscheduled visit from two senior officers, Mr Scanell and Mr Green. To be fair, most meetings in prison are unscheduled; after all, no one calls in advance to fix an appointment with your diary secretary. They are concerned that I am no longer going out into the yard during the afternoon to take advantage of forty-five minutes of fresh air and exercise. They've heard a rumour that on my last outing I was threatened by another prisoner, and for that reason I've remained in my cell. They ask me if this is true, and if so, am I able to supply them with any details of those who threatened me. I tell them exactly what took place in the yard, but add that I am unwilling to name or describe the young tearaway involved. They leave twenty minutes later with several pages of their report sheet left blank.

I ask Tony what would have happened if I'd told them the name of the two culprits.

'They would have been transferred to another prison later today,' Tony replied.

'Wouldn't it be easier for them to transfer me?' I suggest.

'Good heavens, no,' said Tony. 'That would demand a degree of lateral thinking, not to mention common sense.'

6.00 pm

Supper. Vegetable stew and a lollipop. The lollipop was superb.

6.43 pm

Fletch visits my cell and tries to convince me that it's my duty to name the cons who threatened me in the yard, because if I don't, it won't be long before they're doing exactly the same thing to someone less able to take care of themselves. He makes a fair point, but I suggest what the headlines would be the following day if I had given the officers the names: *Archer beaten up in yard; Archer demands extra protection; Under-staffed prison service doing overtime to protect Archer; Archer reports prisoner to screw.* No, thank you, I tell Fletch, I'd rather sit in my cell and write. He sighs, and before leaving, hands me his copy of the *Daily Telegraph.* It's a luxury to have a seventy-two-page paper, even if it is yesterday's. I devour every page.

The lead story is a poll conducted for the *Telegraph* by youGov.com showing that, although Iain Duncan Smith is running 40–60 behind Ken Clarke in the national polls, he is comfortably ahead with the Party membership. It seems to be a no-win situation for the Conservatives. The only person who must be laughing all the way to the voting booth is Tony Blair.

DAY 12

7.08 pm

I have a visit from Paul, a tea-boy – which is why he's allowed to roam around while the rest of us are banged up. He says he has something to tell me, so I pick up my pad, sit on the end of the bed and listen.

Paul is about six foot one, a couple of hundred pounds and looks as if he could take care of himself in a scrap. He begins by telling me that he's just been released from a drug-rehabilitation course at the Princess Diana centre in Norfolk. It's taken them eight months to wean him off his heroin addiction. I immediately enquire if he now considers himself cured. Paul just sits there in silence and avoids answering my question. It's obviously not what he came to talk to me about. He then explains that during his rehab, he was made to write a long self-assessment piece and asks if I will read it, but he insists that no one else on the spur must find out its contents.

'I wouldn't bother you with it,' he adds, 'if it were not for the fact that several prisoners on this spur have had similar experiences, and they're not necessarily the ones you might expect.' He leaves without another word.

If you were to come across Paul at your local, you would assume he was a middle-class successful businessman (he's in jail for credit-card fraud). He's intelligent, articulate and charming. In fact he doesn't look any different to the rest of us, but then why should he? He just doesn't want anyone to know about his past, and I'm not talking about his 'criminal past'.

As soon as my cell door is closed, I begin to read the self-assessment piece that is written in his own hand. He had a happy upbringing until the age of six when his parents divorced. Two years later his mother remarried. After that, he and his brothers were regularly thrashed by their stepfather. The only person he put any trust in was an uncle who befriended him and turned out to be a paedophile. His next revelation I would not consider for a plot in a novel, because it turns out that his uncle is now locked up on House Block Two, convicted of indecent assault on an underaged youth. The two men can see each other through the wire mesh across the yard during the afternoon exercise period. Paul doesn't know what he would do if he were ever to come face to face with his uncle. At no time in his exposition does he offer this as an excuse for his crime, but he points out that child abuse is a common symptom among those serving long-term sentences. I find this quite difficult to come to terms with, having had such a relaxed and carefree upbringing myself. But I decide to ask Fletch if Paul is a) telling the truth, b) correct in his overall assessment.

When I did eventually ask Fletch, I was shocked by his reply.*

10.00 pm

After I've read through Paul's piece a second time, I turn to the latest bunch of letters – just over a hundred – which keep my spirits up, until I switch on the nine o'clock news on Radio 4, to discover that there are still no plans to move me from this hellhole.

11.00 pm

I start to read John Grisham's *The Partner*, and manage seven chapters before turning the light off just after midnight. I can't believe it, no rap music.

---

* This sentence was added two weeks after I had written the original script.

DAY 13   TUESDAY 31 JULY 2001

5.55 am

Woke up before the Alsatians this morning. I've finally worked out why they make so much noise. It's because they are being fed on the same food as the prisoners. Write for two hours.

8.00 am

I finish the box of cornflakes and the last drop of UHT milk, hopeful that my canteen order will materialize at some time later today. I get dressed. I can move another notch up on my belt – I must have lost several pounds, but have no other way of confirming this.

9.00 am

When my cell door is opened, I don't join the other prisoners to go to the workshop as I have an appointment with the Education Assessor, Judy Fitt, known amongst the prisoners as 'Misfit' – a joke she must be heartily sick of.

When Ms Fitt arrives, the officer on the front desk calls for me, or to be more accurate, bellows out my name, as I'm on the top landing, and they never move from the ground floor unless they have to. I go down to meet her. Judy is a short – could lose a few pounds – blonde, of about forty with a happy, optimistic smile. I pick up two chairs from the pile by the TV and place them under the window at the end of the room. I think she's surprised that I insist on carrying her chair. Once seated, she takes me through all the education curriculum has to offer, from teaching reading and writing skills, through to taking a degree. Her enthusiasm leaves me in no doubt that Judy is another public servant dedicated to her job. She also suggests that in my case I could learn to cook, draw, or even, after all these years of avoiding it, discover how to use a computer. That would impress Mary.

I remind Judy that I'm only expecting to be at Belmarsh for a few more days, and would like to use my time to teach other prisoners to read and write. Judy considers this suggestion, but would prefer I gave a creative-writing course, as there are several inmates working on books, poems and essays who will have dozens of unanswered questions. I agree to her request and, aware of my escape plan, Judy suggests I ought to give my first lesson tomorrow morning. She pauses, looking a little embarrassed. 'But first I have to enrol you in the education department.' She passes me over yet more forms. 'Can you complete these tests and let me have them back later today so that I can process them in a matter of hours?'

'I'll try to have them completed by the end of the morning.'

She laughs. 'It won't take you that long.'

I return to my cell, and as I have nothing to do for the thirty minutes before lunch, begin to fill in the little boxes headed Education Test. I've selected some random examples:

DAY 13

1) English – spell these words correctly: wos, befor, wer, gril, migt, siad, affer.
2) Maths –
   a) 13+34, 125+386?
   b) how much change do you get from £5 if you spend £1.20?
3) what is 7.15pm on a twenty-four hour clock?
4) how much time is there between 4.30 and 6.15?
5) what is 25% of 300?
6) if 1 biscuit costs 25p, 6 are £1.38, 12 are £2.64, and 24 are £6, which is the better buy?

I complete the six pages of questions and return them to Ms Fitt, via Billy Little (murder), who has an education class this afternoon.

12 noon

Lunch. Provisions have not yet arrived from the canteen. Half a portion of macaroni cheese and a mug of Highland Spring. Have you noticed I'm beginning to eat prison food?

1.40 pm

My cell door is opened, and I'm told Ms Roberts wants to see me. I am accompanied to the Governor's office by Mr Weedon. I don't bother to ask him why, because he won't know, and even if he does, he wouldn't tell me. Only moments later I discover that Ms Roberts has nothing but bad news to impart and none of it caused by the staff at Belmarsh. My Category D status has been raised to C because the police say they have been left with no choice but to follow up Baroness Nicholson's allegations, and open a full inquiry into what happened to the money raised for the Kurds. As if that wasn't enough, the C-cat prison I've been allocated to is on the Isle of Wight. How much further away do they want me to be from my family?

The raising of my status, Ms Roberts explains, is based on the fear that while a further inquiry is going on I might try to escape. Scotland Yard obviously has a sense of humour. How far do they imagine I could get before someone spotted me?

Ms Roberts informs me that I can appeal against both decisions, and if I do, the authorities have agreed to make an assessment by Thursday. She points out that the Isle of Wight is a long way from my residence in Cambridge, and it's the responsibility of the Home Office to house a prisoner as close to his home as possible. If that's the case, I'm only surprised they're not sending me to the Shetland Isles. She promises to have a word with my solicitor and explain my rights to them. If it were not for Ms Roberts and Ramona Mehta, I would probably be locked up in perpetual solitary confinement.

I cannot express forcibly enough my anger at Emma Nicholson, especially after my years of work for the Kurds. One call to Sir Nicholas Young at the Red Cross and all her questions as to the role I played in the Simple Truth campaign could have been answered. She preferred to contact the press.

Ms Roberts points out that as my lawyers are due to visit me at two o'clock, perhaps I should be making a move. I thank her. Baroness Nicholson could learn a great deal from this twenty-six-year-old woman.

2.00 pm

I join Alex Cameron and Ramona Mehta in the visitors' area. This time we've been allocated a room not much bigger than my cell. But there is a difference – on three sides it has large windows. When you're behind bars day and night, you notice windows.

Before they go on to my appeal against conviction and sentence, I raise three other subjects on which I require legal advice. First, whether the Baroness has stepped over the mark. The lawyers fear she may have worded everything so carefully as to guarantee maximum publicity for herself, without actually accusing me of anything in particular. I point out that I am only too happy to cooperate with any police inquiry, and the sooner the better. The Simple Truth campaign was organized by the Red Cross, and the Treasurer at the time will confirm that I had no involvement whatsoever with the collecting or distributing of any monies. Ramona points out that several Red Cross officials, past and present, have already come out publicly confirming this.

I then tell my lawyers the story of Ali (£28,000 stolen and returned, but now doing an eighteen-month sentence for breach of trust). I ask that the police be reminded that Mrs Peppiatt admitted in the witness box to double-billing, stealing a car, taking her children on a free holiday to Corfu, buying presents for mistresses that didn't exist and claiming expenses for meals with phantom individuals. Can I hope that the CPS will treat her to the same rigorous inspection as Ali and I have been put through?

Third, I remind them that Ted Francis, the man who sold his story to the *News of the World* for fourteen thousand pounds, still owes me twelve thousand. I'd like it back.

The lawyers promise to follow up all these matters. However, they consider the reinstatement of my D-cat and making sure I don't have to go to the Isle of Wight their first priorities.

I ask Ramona to take the next five days of what I've written and hand the script over to Alison for typing up. Ramona leaves our little room to ask the duty officer if he will allow this. He turns down her request. Alex suggests I hold onto the script until I've been transferred to a less security-conscious prison. He also advises me that it would be unwise to think of publishing anything until after my appeal has been considered. I warn them that if I lose my appeal and continue to keep up my present output for the entire sentence, I'll end up writing a million words.

On the hour, an officer appears to warn us that our time is up. Ramona leaves, promising to deal with the problems of my D-cat and the Isle of Wight immediately.

While I'm waiting to be escorted back to Block One, I get into conversation with a Greek Cypriot called Nazraf who is on remand awaiting trial. He's been charged with 'detaining his wife in a motorcar' – I had no idea there was such a charge. I repeat his story here with the usual government health warning. Nazraf tells me that he locked his wife in the car for her own safety because he was at the time transferring a large sum of cash from his place of work to a local bank. He's in the restaurant business and for several years has been very successful, making an annual profit of around £200,000. He adds with some considerable passion that he still loves his wife, and would prefer a reconciliation, but she has already filed for divorce.

Nazraf comes across as a bright, intelligent man, so I have to ask him why he isn't out on bail. He explains that the court demanded a sum of £40,000 to be put up by at least four different people, and he didn't want his friends or business associates to know that he was in any trouble. He had always assumed that the moment he was sent to jail, his wife would come to her senses and drop the charges. That was five weeks ago and she hasn't budged. The trial takes place in mid-September . . .

This is all I could find out before we were released from the waiting room to continue on our separate paths – I to Block One, Nazraf to Block Four. His final destination also puzzles me, because Block Four usually houses terrorists or extremely high-security risks. I'd like to meet Nazraf again, but I have a feeling I never will.

6.00 pm

Supper. Provisions have arrived from the canteen and been left in a plastic bag on the end of my bed. I settle down to a plate of tinned Spam, a bar of Cadbury's Fruit and Nut, two McVitie's digestive biscuits and finally a mug of blackcurrant juice, topped up with Evian water. What more could a man ask for?

8.00 pm

Association. I am asked to join a group of 'more mature' prisoners – at sixty-one I am by far the oldest, if not the most mature – for their weekly committee meeting in Fletch's cell. Other attendees include Tony (marijuana only), Billy (murder), Colin (GBH) and Paul (murder).

Like any well-run board meeting, we have a chairman, Fletch, and an agenda. First we discuss the hours we are permitted to be out of our cells, and how Mr Marsland has made conditions more bearable since he became the senior officer. Fletch considers that relations between the two parties who live on different sides of 'the iron barrier' are far more tenable – even amicable – than at any time in the past. Colin is still complaining about a particular warder, who I haven't yet come across. According to Colin, he treats the prisoners like scum, and will put you on report if you as much as blink in front of him. He's evidently proud of the fact that he's put more people on report than any other officer, and that tells you all you need to know about him, Colin suggests.

I decide to observe this man from a distance and see if Colin's complaint is justified. Most of the officers make an effort 'to keep a lid on things', preferring a calm atmosphere, only too aware that lifers' moods swing from despair to hope and back to despair again in moments. This can, in the hands of an unthinking officer, lead to violence. Colin, I fear, is quick to wrath, and doesn't need to take another step backwards, just as things are going a little better for him.

The next subject the committee discuss is prison finance. Tony reports that the Governor, Hazel Banks, has been given a bonus of £24,000 for bringing Belmarsh Prison costs down by four hundred thousand. Hardly something a free enterprise merchant like myself could grumble about. However, Paul feels the money would have been better spent on inmates' education and putting electricity into the cells. I have no idea if these figures are accurate, but Tony confirms that he checked them in Sir David Ramsbotham's (head of the prison service) annual review.

When the meeting breaks up, Derek Del Boy Bicknell (murder) – interesting that he has not been invited to join the committee meeting – asks if he could have a private word with me. 'I've got something for you to read,' he says. I walk across the ground floor from Cell 9 to Cell 6. After he's offered me a selection of paperbacks, I discover the real reason he wishes to see me.

He wants to discuss his appeal, and produces a letter from his solicitor. The main grounds for his appeal appear to be that his former solicitor advised him not to go into the witness box when he wanted to. He subsequently sacked the solicitor and his QC. He has since appointed a new legal team to advise him, but he's not yet chosen a QC. Imagine my surprise when I discover one of his grounds for appeal is that he is unable to read or write, and therefore never properly understood what his rights were. I look up at a shelf full of books above his bed.

'You can't read?'

'No, but don't tell anyone. You see, I've never really needed to as a car salesman.'

This is a prisoner who carries a great deal of responsibility on the spur. He's a Listener and number one on the hotplate. I earlier described him as a man who could run a private company and I have not changed my mind. Del Boy brings to mind Somerset Maugham's moving short story, 'The Bell Ringer'. However, it's still going to be a disadvantage for him not to be able to study his legal papers. I begin to wonder how many other prisoners fall into the same category, and worse, just won't admit it. I go over the grounds of appeal with Del Boy line by line. He listens intently, but can't make any notes.

8.45 pm

Lock-up is called so I return to my cell to face – delighted to face – another pile of letters left on my bed by Ray the censor. I realize the stack will be even greater tomorrow when the papers inform their readers that I will not be going to an open prison, after Emma Nicholson has dropped her 'I was only doing my duty' barb into an already boiling cauldron.

I've now fallen into a routine, much as I had in the outside world. The big difference is that I have little or no control over when I can and cannot write, so I fit my hours round the prison timetable. Immediately after evening lock-up is designated for reading letters, break, followed by going over my manuscript, break, reading the book of the week, break, undress, go to bed, break, try to ignore the inevitable rap music. Impossible.

Every time I finish the day's script, I wonder if there will be anything new to say tomorrow. However, I'm still on such a steep learning curve, I've nowhere near reached that dizzy height. But I confess I now want to leave Belmarsh for pastures new, and pastures is the key word. I long to walk in green fields and taste fresh air.

Billy (lifer, writer, scholar) tells me it will be better once I've settled somewhere, and don't have to spend my energy wondering when and where I will be for the rest of my sentence. He's been at Belmarsh for two years and seven months, and still doesn't know where he's destined for. Tony (marijuana only, escaped from open prison) warns me that, wherever I go, I'll be quickly bored if I don't have a project to work on. Thankfully, writing these diaries has solved that problem. But for how long?

DAY 14   WEDNESDAY 1 AUGUST 2001

6.21 am

A long, hot, sleepless night. The rap music went on until about four in the morning, so I was only able to doze off for the odd few minutes. When it finally ceased, a row broke out between someone called Mitchell, who I think was in the cell above the music, and another prisoner called Vaz, who owned the stereo below. It didn't take long to learn what Mitchell planned to do to Vaz just as soon as his cell door was opened. Their language bore a faint resemblance to the dialogue in a Martin Amis novel, but without any of his style or panache.

8.37 am

Breakfast. Among my canteen selections is a packet of cereal called Variety, eight different cereals in little boxes. I start off with something called Coco Pops. Not bad, but it's still almost impossible to beat good old Kellogg's Cornflakes.

9.31 am

The morning papers are delivered to the duty officer. They're full of stories confirming that my status has been changed from D-cat to C-cat because of Emma Nicholson's accusations.

9.50 am

Ms Labersham arrives and actually knocks politely on my cell door, as if I were capable of opening it. She unlocks 'the iron barrier' and tells me that she has come to escort me to my creative-writing class.

I'm taken to a smoke-filled waiting room with no chairs, just a table. Well, that's one way of guaranteeing a standing ovation. Moments later a trickle of prisoners appear, each carrying his own plastic chair. Once the nine of them are settled, Ms Labersham reminds everyone that it's a two-hour session. She suggests that I should speak for about an hour and then open it up for a general discussion.

I've never spoken for an hour in my life; it's usually thirty minutes, forty at the most before I take questions. On this occasion I speak for just over forty minutes, explaining how I took up writing at the age of thirty-four after leaving Parliament, with debts of £427,000 and facing bankruptcy. The last time I gave this speech was at a conference in Las Vegas as the principal guest of a US hotel group. They flew me over first class, gave me a suite of rooms and sent me home with a cheque for $50,000.

Today, I'm addressing nine Belmarsh inmates, and Ms Labersham has confirmed that my prison account will be credited with £2 (a bottle of Highland Spring and a tube of toothpaste).

When I've finished my talk, I am surprised how lively the discussion is that follows. One of the prisoners, Michael (aged twenty-one, murder), wants to talk about becoming a song writer, a subject about which I know very little. I don't feel I can tell him that a lyricist is as different to a novelist as a brain surgeon is from a gynaecologist. Michael wants me to read out his latest effort. It's already forty verses in length. I offer you one:

> No room, but to leave
> You call out, calling for me
> to come back
> but all you can hear is the sound of your own voice
> calling out my name

Michael heard yesterday that the judge had given him a tariff of eighteen years.

'At least it's not telephone numbers,' he says.

'Telephone numbers?'

'Nine hundred and ninety-nine years,' he replies.

When I finish reading Michael's work, the group discuss it, before Terry (burglary, former cell-mate) reads three pages of his novel, which he hopes to have finished by the time they release him in December.

The group spend some time debating the use of bad language in a novel. Does it tell you anything about the character the author is writing about? Does it distract from the narrative? They go on to discuss the relative strengths and weaknesses of Terry's story. They don't pull any punches.

Tony (marijuana only) then tells the group that he is writing a textbook on quantum mechanics, which has been a hobby of his for many years. He explains that his efforts will add nothing to the genre – his word – but as a project it keeps him occupied for many hours.

The final rendering is one of Billy Little's poems. It's in a different class to anything we've heard up until then, and everyone in that room knows it.

Crash Bang Slam

Subject despised, committed wrong,
broken wounded, buffeted along,
concealed confined, isolated state,
parental tools, judicial hate.

Golden cuffs, silver chains,
reformed pretence, jewelled pains,
sapphire screams, diamond faults,
brick steel, storage vaults.

Uranium plutonium, nuclear chalice,
poison regimes, political malice,
confounded dark, loomin' sin,
atomised spirits, crushed within.

Seditious dissent, proletarian class,
duplicate religion, misleading mass,
ruinous poverty's, reducing rod,
whipping barbarous, bloodthirsty God.

Liberated justice, equality bound,
desecrating capitalists, unholy ground,
revolutionary concept, militant fire,
diligent radical, poetic desire.

Billy Little (BX7974)

During the last few minutes they begin to discuss when we'll
get together again. The matter that most concerns the group is
whether it should be during Association time or considered as
an education class. On this they are equally divided, and I
wonder if they will ever meet again.

12 noon

Lunch. I open a tin of ham (67p), extract half of it, to which I
add two hard-boiled potatoes (prison issue). During the after-

noon, I devour three digestive biscuits, and swig nearly a whole bottle of Evian. If I continue at this rate, I'll be out of water by Saturday, and like so many prisoners, facing the problem of double-bubble. Do you recall Del Boy cutting a cigarette in half, and expecting a whole one back the following day?

1.07 pm

My appeals against change of status and being sent to the Isle of Wight are brought round to my cell for signing. Ms Taylor says that the Deputy Governor wants the forms returned to her office as soon as possible. I read slowly through the two-page legal document, making only one small emendation. I sign on the dotted line, but remain convinced that the Home Office has already made up its mind, and there is nothing I can do about it. The golden rule seems to be: it mustn't look as if Archer's getting special treatment, even if he's being treated unjustly.

2.24 pm

My cell door is opened by Mr Bentley, who tells me that I must report to reception as there are several parcels for me to collect.

When I leave the spur, I am not searched for the first time and the duty officer simply points to the end of the corridor and says, 'My colleague will guide you.' It's taken them two weeks to feel confident that I have no interest in escaping or dealing in drugs. Actually if you tried to escape from Belmarsh – and the roof is the furthest anyone has managed – you'd need an architect's plan; the whole building is a maze. Even if you work here, I imagine it would take several weeks before you could confidently find your way around. Sometimes I wonder how the prison officers find their way out at night.

At the end of every corridor, a barred gate is opened and I am ushered through it. None of the gatekeepers seem to be surprised that I'm unaccompanied. I finally arrive outside the little cubbyhole called reception. The doors are pulled open to reveal Mr Pearson and Mr Leech.

'Good afternoon, sir,' Mr Pearson says, and then quickly corrects himself, 'Archer. I'm afraid we only have fourteen registered parcels for you this week.' He begins to remove them one by one from the shelves behind him. Half an hour later, I am the proud owner of four more Bibles, three copies of the New Testament, and a prayer book. I retain one copy of the New Testament, which is leather-bound, as I feel Terry would appreciate it. I suggest to Mr Leech that the rest should be sent to Mr Powe at the chapel. The other packages consist of three novels, two scripts and a proposal of marriage from a blonde woman of about fifty, who adds that if I don't fancy her, she has a daughter of twenty-four (photo enclosed).

I've considered printing her 'Dear Geoffrey,' (sic) letter and photograph, but my solicitors have advised against it.

When they've opened the final package on the shelf, I point to a box of tissues and ask, 'Are those also mine by any chance?'

Mr Pearson looks at Mr Leech, and says, 'I think they are.'

He passes across two boxes of tissues, making the whole expedition worthwhile.

Mr Pearson accompanies me – I say accompanies, because I didn't get the feeling of being escorted – back to my cell. En route he tells me that the prison was built ten years ago by a Canadian architect and it's all right-angles.

'It might have been more sensible,' he mutters, 'to have consulted serving prison officers, and then we could have pointed out the problems staff and inmates come up against

DAY 14

every day.' Before I can offer an opinion, I find myself locked
back in my cell.

2.57 pm

I've only been in my cell for a few minutes when Mr Weedon
reappears bearing a slip of paper. It's a movement schedule,
confirming my worst fears. I will be transferred to the Isle of
Wight sometime during the week of 6 August 2001. (See
opposite.) It is as I thought; the Home Office have made up their
minds, and are unwilling to take any personal needs into con-
sideration. I sink onto my bed, depressed. I am helpless, and
there's nothing I can do about it.

3.14 pm

I'm writing the second draft of today's script, when the alarm
bell goes off. I can hear running feet, raised voices and the
scurrying of prison officers. I look out of my barred window but
can see nothing but an empty yard. I gaze through the four-by-
nine-inch slit in my door, and quickly realize that the commotion is not on our spur. I'll have to wait for Association before I
can find out what happened.

4.00 pm

Association. Once again, I fail to get on the gym rota and suspect
it's the same eight inmates who are pre-selected every day, and I
haven't been a member of the club long enough to qualify. Let's
hope they have a bigger gym on the Isle of Wight.

When I reach the ground floor, I see that Fletch is placed
strategically in one corner, as he is at the beginning of every

NOTIFICATION OF TRANSFER

1-1-3

NAME...ARCHER...

NUMBER..FF8282..

This is to advise you that you are provisionally due to be transferred to
HMP....CAMPHILL
This transfer will take place during the week beginning...06-08-01

If you have relevant reasons that you feel you cannot be transferred, please discuss the problem with your Houseblock Senior Officer.

Association, in case anyone needs to seek his help or advice. I slip across and have a word.

'What was all the noise about?' I ask.

'A fight broke out on Block Two.'

'Any details?'

'Yes, some con called Vaz has been playing rap music all night, and the man in the cell above him hasn't slept for three days.'

'He has my sympathy,' I tell Fletch.

'They didn't come face to face until this afternoon,' continues Fletch, 'when Mitchell, who was in the cell above, not only laid out Vaz with one punch, but set fire to his cell and ended up jumping on top of his stereo.' Fletch paused. 'It was one of those rare occasions when the prison staff took their time to reach the scene of the crime; after all, they'd received several complaints during the week from other prisoners concerning "the Vaz attitude problem".'

'What happened to the other guy?'

'Mitchell?' said Fletch. 'Officially banged up in segregation, but they'll be moving him to another wing tomorrow; after all, as I explained to Mr Marsland, he was doing no more than representing the views of the majority of inmates.' Another insight into how prison politics work, with Fletch acting as the residents' spokesman.

Billy Little (murder) asks me if I can join him in his cell to discuss a paper he's writing on globalization. He wants to discuss the BBC; its role and responsibility as a public broadcaster. He produces a graph to show how its viewing figures dropped by 4 per cent between 1990 and 1995, and another 4 per cent between 1995 and 2000. I tell Billy that I suspect Greg Dyke, the new Director General, having spent his working life in commercial television, will want to reverse that trend. The beneficiaries,

Billy goes on to tell me, giving detailed statistics, are Sky Digital and the other digital TV stations. Their graphs have a steady upward trend.

I ask Billy when he will have completed his degree course. He removes a sheet of paper from a file below the window. 'September,' he replies.

'And then what?' I ask.

'I may take your advice and write a novel. I've no idea if I can do it, but the judge certainly gave me enough time to find out.'

I can't always pick up every word this Glaswegian utters, but I'm deciphering a few more syllables each day. I've decided to ask Alison to send him a copy of Vikram Seth's *A Suitable Boy*. I consider it's exactly the type of work Billy would appreciate, especially as it was Mr Seth's first novel, so he'll discover what he's up against.

When I leave him, the pool table is occupied, the queue for the two telephones is perpetual, and the afternoon film is *Carry on Camping*. I return to my cell, door unlocked, and continue writing.

6.00 pm

Supper. I risk a vegetable fritter and two prison potatoes (three mistakes). I continue to drink my bottled water as if I have an endless supply (the temperature today is 91°). Double-bubble is fast looming, and I'll need to see Del Boy fairly soon if I am to survive. As I move down the hotplate, Andy (murder) slips two chocolate ice-creams onto my tray. 'Put one in your pocket,' he whispers. Now I discover what the word treat really means. Del Boy is standing at the other end of the counter in his role as number one hotplate man. An official title. As I pass the custard pie, I ask if we could meet up later. He nods. He can smell when someone's in trouble. As a Listener, Derek is allowed to visit any cell if another inmate needs to discuss a personal problem. And I have a personal problem. I'm running out of water.

7.00 pm

I settle down to go over my script for the day before turning to the post. The pattern continues unabated, but to my surprise, few mention the Kurds. Paul (credit-card fraud) told me when I was queuing up at the canteen that *The Times* had made it clear that I had no involvement with the collecting or distributing of any monies. That had been the responsibility of the Red Cross. However, there was one letter in the pile that didn't fall into any of the usual slots.

I have now been locked up in a Category A, high-security prison for two weeks, which I share with thirty-two murderers, and seventeen other lifers mainly convicted of attempted murder or manslaughter; I've lost my mother, who I adored; I've been incarcerated on the word of a man who colluded with the *News of the World* to set me up, and by a woman who is a self-confessed thief; and I'm about to be sent to the Isle of Wight, a C-cat prison, because of the word of Baroness Nicholson. So I confess I had to chuckle, a rare event recently, when I received the following missive. (See opposite.)

8.40 pm

My cell door is unlocked by an officer and Del Boy is allowed to join me. His smile is as wide as ever, as he strolls in looking like a rent collector visiting someone who doesn't always pay on time. He takes a seat on the end of the bed. For some time we

Chan's Optometrist

Mr J Archer   Mr Kenneth Chan BSc. MCOptom.
Belmarsh House   90 High Street
Belmarsh   Lee-on-Solent
South East London   Hampshire
                               PO13 9DA
                               31/7/2001

Dear Mr. Archer

I am sorry to trouble you. The reason I write to you is because one of my patients like your spectacles (The rimless pair you wore when you went to the funeral). I would be most grateful if you can let me know the brand, the model number, the colour and the size of the frame. All these information should be printed on the sides of the frame. Your reply will be appreciated.

Thank you for your attention!

Yours Sincerely,

K. Chan.

discuss his upcoming appeal and the fact that he cannot read or write. It transpires that he can make out the odd word if he concentrates, but can only sign his name.

'I've never needed much more,' he explains. 'I'm a barrow boy, not a banker.'

He makes a fair point, because were you to close your eyes and listen to him speak, although he's quite unable to hide his cockney upbringing you certainly wouldn't know he was black. He promises to take reading lessons just as soon as I depart for the Isle of Wight. I'm not convinced he'll ever find out which floor the education department is on, until the curriculum includes 'double-bubble'.

'Now how can I help?' he asks. 'Because I'm the man.'

'Well, if you're the man, Derek, I'm running out of water, among other things.'

'No problem,' he replies, 'and what are the other things?'

'I'd like three bottles of Highland Spring, two packets of McVitie's chocolate biscuits and a tube of toothpaste.'

'No problem,' he repeats. 'They'll be delivered to your cell in the morning, squire.'

'And no double-bubble?'

'No double-bubble.' He hesitates. 'As long as you agree never to say anything because if anyone found out it wouldn't do my reputation any good.'

'No problem,' I hear myself saying.

On the outside, in that world I have vacated, a handful of people can make things happen. The secret is to know that handful of people. It's no different on the inside. Derek 'Del Boy' Bicknell is a natural Chief Whip, Fletch, the Leader of the Opposition, Billy, Secretary of State for Education, Tony, Chancellor of the Exchequer, Paul, Home Secretary, and Colin, Secretary of State for Defence. Wherever you are, in whatever circumstances, leadership will always emerge. Block One, spur one, houses thirty-two murderers, seventeen lifers, and, without realizing it, has formed an inmates' Cabinet. Nothing on paper, nothing official, but it works.

After Derek departs, I settle down on my bed to finish John Grisham's *The Partner*. It's too long, but what a storyteller.

10.07 pm

I put my head on the pillow. I can scarcely believe it, no more rap music. Well done, Mitchell.

DAY 15   THURSDAY 2 AUGUST 2001

5.51 am

A full night's sleep. For the first time I can hear the cars on the road in the distance. I write for two hours, interrupted only by the occasional bark of an Alsatian.

8.00 am

Breakfast. Frosties and long-life milk (second day).

9.00 am

Association. I remind Derek of my acute water-shortage problem. Now down to half a bottle. It's all under control, he claims.

I line up with the other prisoners for the gym.

Derek Jones (GBH, artist) spots me on the middle corridor and tells me that he did a spell at Camphill on the Isle of Wight. I quiz him, and discover that it has a fully equipped gym, one of the best in the country (by that he means in prisons), but he adds alarmingly that, 'It's full of shit-heads and scum. Young tearaways who think of themselves as gangsters because they've robbed some old lady. No one on the spur understands why you're being sent there.' I panic, desert the queue for the gym, run upstairs, grab my phonecard, rush back down and call Alison.

First I warn her (no time for pleasantries when you only have twenty units on your weekly card) that the next five days of the script are on their way, and to let Ramona know when they have arrived so she can confirm this on her next legal visit. I then ask to be put through to James. My younger son has assumed the role of joint head of the household in charge of finance, while William's responsibility is to take care of his mother. I don't lose a moment's sleep wondering if they're up to it. I quickly tell Jamie about the Isle of Wight and the loss of my D-cat status.

'Calm down, Dad,' he says. 'We've been working on little else for the past forty-eight hours. I know how you must feel being so out of touch, but we're on the case. Ramona spoke to the Home Office last night, and they're hinting that it's unlikely that there will even be an inquiry into the Kurdish matter. No one is taking Nicholson's accusations seriously, even the tabloids have ignored her.'

'Yes, but these things still take time; meanwhile I've been issued with a movement order.'

'The same source,' James continues, 'is hinting that you're more likely to end up in the home counties, but they're still working on it.'

I check my phonecard; I've already used six units. 'Anything else?' I ask. I want to save as many units as possible for Mary on Sunday.

'Yes, I need your authority to transfer some dollars into your sterling account. The pound has been off for the past couple of days.'

'That's fine by me,' I tell him.

'By the way,' he says, 'lots of people are talking about the judge's summing-up, so chin up. Bye, Dad.'

I put the phone down to find I have used seven of my twenty units. I leave James to worry about the currency market while I concentrate on trying to get my hands on a bottle of Highland Spring.

I check my watch. No point in returning to the gym queue, so I settle for a shower. You forget how dirty you are, until you discover how clean you can be.

11.00 am

The officer on the front desk bellows out, 'Exercise,' which once again I avoid. It's 92° out there in the yard, with no shade. I elect to sit in my cell, writing, with the tiny window as wide open as I can force it. When I've completed ten pages of script, I switch on the Test Match. The game is only an hour old, and England are 47 for 2.

12 noon

Lunch. I pick up my tray and walk down to the hotplate, but can't find a single item I would offer an emaciated dog. I leave with a piece of buttered bread and an apple. Back in my cell I tuck into the other half of my tin of Prince's ham, two more McVitie's digestive biscuits, and a mug of water. I try to convince myself that Del Boy is the man, and he will deliver – in the nick of time – because there's only two inches left in the bottle. Have you ever had to measure how much water is left in a bottle?

2.00 pm

An officer appears outside my cell door and orders me to report to the workshop, which I'm not enthusiastic about. After all, my application for education must surely have been processed by now. When I arrive at the bubble on the centre floor to join the other prisoners, I'm searched before having my name ticked off. We are then escorted down a long corridor to our different destinations – workshop and education. When we reach the end of the corridor, prisoners destined for the workshop turn left, those with higher things on their mind, right. I turn right.

When I arrive at education, I walk past a set of classrooms with about six or seven prisoners in each; a couple of prison officers are lounging around in one corner, while a lady sitting behind a desk on the landing crosses off the names of inmates before allocating them to different classrooms. I come to a halt in front of her.

'Archer,' I tell her.

She checks down the list, but can't find my name. She looks puzzled, picks up a phone and quickly discovers that I ought to be in the workshop.

'But Ms Fitt told me I would be processed for education immediately.'

'Strange word, immediately,' she says. 'I don't think anyone at Belmarsh has looked up its meaning in the dictionary, and until they do I'm afraid you'll have to report to the workshops.' I can't imagine what the words 'until they do' mean. I retrace my steps, walking as slowly as I can in the direction of the workshops, and find I am the last to arrive.

This time I'm put on the end of the chain gang – a punishment for being the last to turn up. My new, intellectually challenging job is to place two small packets of margarine, one sachet of raspberry jam, and one of coffee into a plastic bag before it's sealed up and taken away for use in another prison. The young man opposite me who is sealing up the bags and then dropping them into a large cardboard box looks like a wrestler. He's about five foot ten, early twenties, wears a spotless white T-shirt and smart designer jeans. His heavily muscled arms are bronzed, so it's not difficult to work out that he hasn't been in Belmarsh that long. The answer to that question turns out to be three weeks. He tells me that his name is Peter. He's married with one child and runs his own company.

'What do you do?' I ask.

'I'm a builder.' When a prisoner say's 'I'm' something, and not 'I used to be' something, then you can almost be certain that their sentence is short or they're on remand. Peter goes on to tell me that he and his brother run a small building company that specializes in buying dilapidated houses in up-and-coming areas of Essex. They renovate the houses and then sell them on. Last year, between them, they were able to earn around two thousand pounds a week. But that was before Peter was arrested. He comes across as a hard-working, decent sort of man. So what's he doing in Belmarsh? I ask myself. Who can he possibly have murdered? His brother, perhaps? He answers that question without my having to enquire.

'I was caught driving my brother's van without a licence. My brother usually does the driving, but he was off sick for the day, so I took his building tools from the work site to my home and for that the judge sentenced me to six weeks in jail.'

Let me make it clear. I have no objection to the sentence, but it's madness to have sent this man to Belmarsh. I do hope that the Home Secretary, Mr Blunkett – who I know from personal dealings when John Major was Prime Minister to be a decent, caring man – will read the next page carefully.

'Are you in a cell on your own?' I enquire.

'No, I'm locked up with two other prisoners.'

'What are they in for?'

'One's on a charge of murder awaiting his trial, the other's a convicted drug dealer.'

'That can't be much fun,' I say, trying to make light of it.

Are you still with me, Home Secretary?

'It's hell,' Peter replies. 'I haven't slept for more than a few minutes since the night they sent me here. I just can't be sure what either of them might get up to. I can handle myself, but the two men I'm sharing a cell with are professional criminals.'

Are you still paying attention, Home Secretary?

'And worse,' he adds. 'One of them offered me a thousand pounds to beat up a witness before his trial begins.'

'Oh, my God,' I hear myself say.

'And he's putting more and more pressure on me each day. Of course I wouldn't consider such an idea, but I've still got another three days to go, and I'm beginning to fear that I might not be safe even when I get out.'

Home Secretary, this hard-working family man is fearful for his own safety. Is that what you're hoping to achieve for someone who's been caught driving without a licence?

I've received over a thousand letters of support since I arrived a Belmarsh and even at sixty-one I have found prison a difficult experience to come to terms with. Peter is twenty-three, with his whole life ahead of him. Hundreds of people are being sent to this Category A top-security prison who should never be here.

But what can I do about it? I can hear the Home Secretary asking one of his officials.

Classify anyone who is arrested as A, B, C or D before their trial begins, not after. Then, if they're D-cat – first-time offenders with no record of violence – they can, if convicted, be sent direct to an open prison. That way they won't have to share cells with murderers, drug dealers or professional criminals. And don't listen to officials when they tell you it can't be done. Sack them, and do it. I was allocated D-cat status within twenty-four hours because of my mother's funeral, so I know it can be done.

Home Secretary, you are doing irreparable damage to decent people's lives and you have no right to do so.

While I'm trying to take in Peter's plight, the pile of plastic bags has grown into a mountain in front of me. Another prisoner who I hadn't noticed before, obviously an old lag, slots quickly into the one position that ensures the chain moves back into full swing.

'This place is more about retribution than rehabilitation, wouldn't you say, Jeffrey?' What is it about the Irish that always makes you relax and feel you've known them all your life? I nod my agreement. He smiles, and introduces himself as William Keane.

Before I repeat what William told me during the next couple of hours, I must warn you that I haven't a clue how much of his tale can be authenticated, but if only half of it is true, God help the Prime Minister, the Home Secretary, the Secretary of State for Health and the Education Secretary.

William was born in Limerick, son of a prize fighter (Ireland must be the last country on earth that still has prize fighters) and a local beauty – William is a handsome man. Mrs Keane produced seven sons and five daughters.

Now William's accent is quite difficult to follow, so I often have to ask him to repeat whole sentences. His present home is a few hundred yards from the prison, so family visits are not a problem. It's the family that's the problem. One of them, the youngster, as William describes him, is on the far bench – marmalade and jam sachets – and at some point, William tells me, all seven brothers and one sister were in jail at the same time, serving sentences between them of one hundred and twelve years. I can only feel sorry for their mother.

William is completing a ten-year sentence for drug dealing, and has only twelve weeks left to serve. You notice he doesn't say three months, because three months would mean thirteen weeks.

He's actually quite fearful about how the world will have changed when in October he steps out of prison for the first time in a decade. He flatters me, a natural pastime for the Irish, by saying he's read all my books, as it seems half the leading criminals in England have.

During his time in six prisons (he's a post-graduate on such establishments), William has taken a degree, and read over four hundred books – I only point this out to make you aware that we are not dealing with a fool. He adds his condolences over my mother's death, and asks how the police and prison staff dealt with me when it came to the funeral. I tell him that they couldn't have been more thoughtful and considerate.

'Not like my brother's funeral,' he says. 'Not only were the whole family in handcuffs, but they had helicopters circling overhead. There were more police by the graveside than mourners.'

'But in my case,' I pointed out, 'no one thought I would try to escape.'

'Houdini couldn't have escaped from that bunch,' William retorts.

What puzzles me about William is that if the rest of the

173

family are as bright and charismatic as he is, why don't they combine their talents and energy and do something worthwhile, rather than settling for a life of crime?

'Drugs,' he replies, matter-of-factly. 'Once you're hooked, you can never earn enough to satisfy the craving, so you end up becoming either a thief or a pusher. And I have to admit,' William adds, 'I'm lazy.'

I've watched him carefully since he's joined the chain, and the one thing he is not, is lazy. He has filled more plastic bags than Peter and me put together. I point this out to him.

'Well, when I say lazy, Jeffrey, I mean lazy about settling down to a nine-to-five job, when you can pick up a couple of grand a week selling drugs.'

'So will you go back to the drug scene once you're released?'

'I don't want to,' he says. 'I'm thirty-five, and one thing's for certain, I don't need to come back inside.' He hesitates. 'But I just don't know if I'm strong-willed enough to stay away from drugs or the quick rewards that are guaranteed when you sell them.'

'How much are we talking about,' I ask, 'and which drugs in particular?'

'Heroin,' he says, 'is the biggest money-spinner. A joey' – even after an explanation, I'm still not quite sure what a joey is – 'has come down in price from one hundred pounds to forty since I've been in prison [ten years], which is a clear indication how the market has grown. And some people need as many as ten joeys a day. When I first came into prison,' William continues, 'cocaine was the designer drug. Today it's heroin, and it's often your lot who are on it,' he says, looking directly at me.

'But I've never taken a drug in my life,' I tell him, 'I don't even smoke.'

'I knew that the moment you walked in,' he said.

'How can you be so sure?'

'The first thing I check is the pallor of the skin – not bad for sixty-one,' he says, displaying that Irish charm again. 'Then I look at the nose, followed by the lips and finally the arms, and it's clear you're not a potential customer. But I'd be willing to bet there's something you need Del Boy to supply you with.'

'Bottled water, still, preferably Highland Spring.'

'How many bottles do you order from the canteen?'

'Four, maybe five a week.'

'Don't let the screws find out.'

'Why not? I pay for them.'

'Because while cannabis and cocaine remain in your bloodstream for a month, heroin can be flushed out in twenty-four hours. If it wasn't you, Jeffrey, the screws would assume you were a heroin addict trying to show up negative whenever you were called in for a Mandatory Drug Test, and it's all the fault of Ann Widdecombe.'

'How can it possibly be Ann Widdecombe's fault?'

'Because it was Widdecombe who first brought in the MDT. That single decision has turned some cannabis smokers into heroin addicts.'

'That's quite a quantum leap,' I suggest, 'and some accusation.'

'No,' says William, 'it was inevitable, and it only happened because Widdecombe knew nothing about the drug culture in prisons. How could she? Neither did you, before you were sent to Belmarsh. And worse, no one seems to have explained the problem to Blunkett either, because both are indirectly responsible for an unnecessary rise in heroin addicts, and even in some cases their deaths.'

'Hold on,' I say. 'That's accusing Blunkett and Widdecombe of manslaughter and cannot be either fair or accurate.'

'When you take an MDT, they test you for marijuana [cannabis], cocaine, crack cocaine and heroin,' continues William, ignoring my comment. 'It's a urine test, and your sample is sent to an independent laboratory and then returned to the prison a week later with the result.'

'I'm with you so far.'

'Marijuana can show up in urine for as long as twenty-eight days. You may well have smoked a joint three weeks ago, even forgotten about it, but it will still come up as positive on an MDT, which is not the case with heroin. Because if you drink pints of water immediately after taking the drug, you can clear any trace of heroin out of your system within twenty-four hours, which means you won't test positive.'

Pay attention, Home Secretary.

'If the test comes back positive for marijuana, the Governor can add twenty-eight days to your sentence and take away all your privileges. Twenty-eight days for one joint,' says William. 'So in prison some marijuana smokers who are on short sentences turn to heroin as an alternative because there's less chance of their sentence being lengthened. Result? They often leave prison as heroin addicts, having never touched a hard drug on the outside. Fact: a percentage of them die within weeks of being released. Why? Because the heroin in prison is considerably weaker compared with the gear you can get "on the out", which causes them to overdose when they inject the same amount. This is a direct result of government legislation.'

'So what would you do about it?' I ask.

'The Mandatory Drug Test should be for Class A and B drugs only [heroin, cocaine], not for marijuana.* This simple decision

---

* Since this was written, the Home Secretary has downgraded cannabis/marijuana to Class C classification.

would cut down the desire to experiment with heroin among twenty per cent of the prison population and would also save countless lives. If any your officials are stupid enough to suggest this isn't true, Home Secretary, tell them not to rely simply on statistics, but to spend a few weeks in prison where they'll quickly find out the truth.'

'I presume, however, it is true that drugs are the direct cause of our prisons being so overcrowded?'

'Yes, but it's a myth that heroin is the main cause of street crime. Crack cocaine is just as much of a problem for the police.' I don't interrupt. 'Crack cocaine,' William continues, 'is for crack-heads, and is far more dangerous than heroin. If you take cocaine you are immediately satisfied, and can be on a high after only one dose, and as you come off it, you may well fall asleep. If you take *crack* cocaine, once you've run out of your supply, you'll do anything to get your hands on some more to prolong the experience. It's the crack-cocaine addicts that rob old ladies of their handbags and young girls of their mobile phones, not heroin addicts; they're more likely to beg, borrow or shoplift. The problem the government hasn't acknowledged is that Britain is now the crack-cocaine capital of Europe, and if you want to set up an award for European drugs city of the year, you wouldn't have to look any further than Bradford. That city would win first prize, year in and year out.'

'Do you have a solution to the problem?' I ask.

'We should go down the Swiss route,' William suggests. 'They register addicts, who can report to a doctor and immediately become part of a detox programme and get their fix of methadone or subitrex. The Swiss recently held a referendum on the issue and the public voted overwhelmingly in favour of the registration of drug addicts and tackling the problem head-on. Result: street crime has fallen by 68 per cent.'

Well, what do you know, Mr Blunkett?

'Do you also want to learn about the National Health detox programme?' asks William. I nod. 'If you're a heroin addict "on the out" and report your addiction to a local GP, it will take you eight to ten weeks to get yourself registered. However, if you commit a crime and are sent to prison, you don't have to wait, because you'll be put on a detox programme the following morning.' William pauses. 'I've known addicts who've committed a crime simply to ensure they get themselves into prison and onto detox overnight.'

What about that, Home Secretary?

'And worse,' William continues, 'most of the addicts "on the out" who go as far as getting themselves registered, fail to turn up ten weeks later to begin the course, because by then they've either lost interest, or are too far gone to care.'

Enter the Secretary of State for Health.

William looks around the room at the fifty or so workers packing their little plastic bags. 'I can tell you every one in this room who's on drugs, even the gear they're on, and it often only takes a glance. And you'd be surprised how many of your friends "on the out", even one or two of those who have been condemning you recently, are among them.'

'Taking cannabis can hardly be described as a major crime,' I suggest. 'My bet is it will be decriminalized in the not too distant future.'

'I'm not talking about cannabis, Jeffrey. The biggest crisis the government is facing today is the rapid growth of heroin addicts. I can name three lords, two Members of Parliament, and two television personalities who are on Class A drugs. I know because a member of my family has been supplying them for years.' He names all of them. Two I already knew about, but the other five come as a surprise. 'In theory they should all be in jail along with you,' he adds. Check on all the young criminals coming into prison and you'll begin to understand it's a problem that few people, especially the politicians, seem willing to face up to. 'On your own spur alone,' he continues, 'five of the lifers are on heroin, and still getting the skag delivered to them every week.'

'How do they manage that?' I ask.

'Mainly during visits,' he says, 'mouth, backside, ears, even secreted in a woman's hair. Because of the Human Rights Act, prison searches are fairly cursory.'

'But this is a Double A Category high-security prison,' I remind him.

'That's not a problem if you're desperate enough, and there's nothing more desperate than a heroin addict, even when he's locked up in the segregation block.'

'But how?' I press him.

'Don't forget that most A cats are also remand prisons, and so have prisoners coming in and out every day. If the new young criminals didn't already know, it wouldn't take them long to discover the economics of supply and demand, especially when such large sums of money are involved. A gram of heroin [a joey] may be worth forty pounds on the street, but in here it can be split up into five bags and sold for a couple of hundred. At those prices, some prisoners are willing to risk swallowing a bag of heroin just before they're taken down; then they simply have to wait to retrieve it; after all, there's a toilet in every cell. And,' he adds, 'my brother Rory can swallow a lump of heroin the size of a small eraser – five hundred pounds in value – hold it in his throat and still carry on a conversation. As soon as he's safely back in his cell, he coughs it up.'

'But despite your brother's unusual skill,' I point out, 'if, as you suggest, sixty per cent of inmates are on drugs, you'll need more than the odd prisoner who's willing to swallow a packet of heroin to satisfy the demand.'

'True,' said William, 'so stay alert during visits, Jeffrey, and you'll notice how much transferring of drugs is done by kissing. And whenever you see a baby dangling on its mother's knee, you can be sure the little offspring's nappy will be full of drugs. That's how the visitor gets it into prison. The kissing is how it's transferred from visitor to inmate. And there are still a dozen or more ways of getting the gear in, depending on which prison you're sent to. If you ever spot someone coming into jail wearing an Adidas tracksuit, look carefully at the three stripes. If you unstitch just one of them, you can fill it with five hundred pounds' worth of heroin.'

My only thought is that I have an Adidas tracksuit in my cell.

'My brother Michael,' continues William, 'discovered that in some prisons Waterstone's have the book franchise, so a friend of his would select an obscure title, fill the spine with drugs, and then ask Waterstone's to donate the book to the prison library. Once it had been placed on the shelf, Michael would take it out. Amazing how much heroin you can get into the spine of James Joyce's *Ulysses*. But in my last nick,' William continues, 'the *Sun*'s page-three girl was the most popular method of getting the skag in, until the screws caught on.'

'The page-three girl?'

'You do know what a page-three girl is, don't you, Jeffrey?' I nod. 'Most A- and B-cat prisons allow an inmate to order a morning paper from the local newsagent,' continues William, 'and because you're locked up for twenty-two hours a day, they even deliver them to your cell. One enterprising dealer "on the out" supplied the entire prison's needs, by sprinkling any orders all over the page-three girl in the *Sun*. He would then cut out another copy of the same photograph and seal it carefully over her twin, making a thin bag of heroin. He ended up supplying a grand's worth of heroin a day to one prison, with an officer unwittingly delivering his wares to the customer direct. He was making far more with his built-in customers than he could ever hope to make "on the out".'

'But how did he get paid?'

'Oh, Jeffrey, you're so green. On every spur, on every block, in every prison, you'll find a dealer who has a supplier on the outside and he'll know your needs within hours of your being locked up.'

'But that doesn't answer my question.'

'You make an order with your spur dealer,' continues William, 'say a gram of heroin a day. He then tells you the name and address of his supplier, and you select someone "on the out" to handle the payments. No standing orders, you understand, just cash. In your case you could have your supply delivered under the Scarfe cartoon in the *Sunday Times*.' I laugh 'Or under the stamps on one of those large brown envelopes you receive every day. You'd be surprised how much cocaine you can deposit under four postage stamps. You watch the screws when the post arrives in the morning. They always run a thumb over the stamps, but you can get a lot more in via the envelope.'

'But they always slit the envelopes open and look inside.'

'I didn't say inside,' said William. 'You may have noticed that down the right-hand side of most brown envelopes there's a flap, which, if you lift carefully, you can fill with heroin and then seal back down again. I know a man who has *Motor Magazine* sent in every week, but it's under the flap of the brown envelope that he's getting his weekly fix.'

'As soon as the buzzer goes, I'm going to have to run back to my cell and write all this down,' I tell him.

'How do you write your books?' William enquires.

'With a felt-tip pen.'

'Lift the cap off the bottom and you can get about fifty pounds' worth of crack cocaine stuffed in there, which is why the screws make you buy any writing implements direct from the canteen.'

'Keep going,' I say, having long ago given up sealing any plastic bags, but somehow William manages to do that job for me as well.

'The most outrageous transfer I've ever seen was a twenty-seven-stone con who hid the drugs under the folds of his skin, because he knew no officer would want to check.'

'But they must have machines to do the checking for them?'

'Yes, they do, in fact vast sums have been spent on the most sophisticated machinery, but they only identify razor blades, guns, knives, even ammunition, but not organic substances. For that, they have to rely on dogs, and a nappy full of urine will put even the keenest bloodhound off the scent.'

'So visits are the most common way of bringing in drugs?'

'Yes, but don't assume that lawyers, priests or prison officers are above being carriers, because when they turn up for legal and religious visits, or in the case of officers, for work, they are rarely searched. In some cases lawyers are paid their fees from drugs delivered to their clients. And when it comes to letters, if they're legal documents, the envelope has to be opened in front of you, and the screws are not allowed to read the contents. And while you're standing in front of a screw, he's less likely to check under the stamps or the side flaps. By the way, there's a legal shop in Fleet Street that is innocently supplying envelopes with the words LEGAL DOCUMENT, *Strictly Private and Confidential* printed on the top left-hand corner. Several drug dealers have a monthly supply of such envelopes, and the only time they ever see a court is when they are standing in the dock.'

'You also mentioned priests?'

'Yes, I knew a Sikh giani [priest] at Gartree who used to give his blessing once a week in a prisoner's cell from where he supplied the entire Sikh community with drugs.'

'How did he manage that?'

'They were secreted in his turban. Did you know that a turban can be eighteen feet of material? You can tuck an awful lot of drugs in there.' William pauses. 'Though in his case, one of his flock grassed on him, and he ended up doing a seven year bird.'

'And prison officers?'

'Screws are paid around three hundred pounds a week, and can pick up another thirteen pounds an hour overtime. Think about it. A half-dozen joeys of heroin and they can double their wages. I knew a member of the kitchen staff at my last prison who brought the stuff in once a week in his backpack.'

'But he would have been liable to a random search at any time?'

'True,' William replied, 'and they did regularly search his backpack, but not the shoulder straps.'

'But if they get caught?'

'They end up on the other side of the bars for a long stretch. We've got a couple in here right now, but they'll shift them out to D-cats before it becomes common knowledge.' He pauses. 'For their own safety. But the championship,' says William, like any good storyteller holding the best until last, 'goes to Harry, the amateur referee from Devon.' By now, William has a captive audience, as all the workers on our table have stopped depositing their wares into little plastic bags as they hang on his every word. 'Harry,' continues William, 'used to visit his local prison once a week to referee a football match. His contact was the goalkeeper, and at the end of each game, both men would return to the changing room, take off their boots and put on trainers. They would then leave carrying the other person's boots. There was enough heroin packed into the referee's hollow studs for him to buy a country cottage after only a couple of seasons. And remember, every match has to be played at home. There are no away fixtures for prisoners. However, the silly man got greedy and started filling up the football as well. He's currently serving a ten-year sentence in Bristol.'

'So where does the dealer get his supplies from?' I ask William as the hands of the clock edge nearer and nearer towards twelve, and I am fearful we may never meet again.

'They're picked up for him by mules.'

'Mules?'

'The dealer often recruits university students who are already hooked – probably by him. He'll then send them on an all-expenses-paid holiday to Thailand, Pakistan or even Colombia and give them an extra thousand pounds if they can smuggle a kilo of heroin through customs.'

'How big is a kilo?'

'A bag of sugar.'

'And what's it worth?'

'The dealer passes on that kilo for around £28,000–£35,000 to sellers, known as soldiers. The soldiers then add baking powder and brick dust until they have four kilos, which they sell on in grams or joeys* for forty pounds a time to their customers. A top soldier can make a profit of seventy to a hundred thousand pounds a month. And don't forget, Jeff, it's cash, so they won't

---

* A joey is about the size of two aspirins.

end up paying any tax, and with that kind of profit there are a lot of punters out there willing to take the risk. The heroin on sale at King's Cross or Piccadilly,' William continues, 'will usually be about four to seven per cent pure. The heroin that the mule brings back from an all-expenses-paid holiday could be as high as 92 per cent pure. By the way,' he adds, 'if the soldiers didn't dilute their wares – cut the smack – they'd kill off most of their customers within a week.'

'How many heroin addicts are there in this country?' I ask.

'Around a quarter of a million,' William replies, 'so it's big business.'

'And how many of those . . .'

A buzzer goes to alert the prison staff that the work period is over, and in a few moments we will be escorted back to our cells. William says, 'It's nice to have met you, Jeffrey. Give my regards to your wife – a truly remarkable woman. Sorry about the judge. Strange that he preferred to believe the word of someone who admitted in court to being a thief. But whatever you do, keep writing the books, because however long you live, there's always going to be a Keane in jail.'

William offers me one final piece of advice before we part. 'I know you've been attending chapel on Sundays, but try the RCs this week. Father Kevin preaches a fine sermon, and you'll like him.'

I walk back to my cell, delighted to have missed education, having spent two hours being educated.

On the route march back to my cell I'm joined by Ali (breach of trust, stole £28,000 from his employer, gave it all back), who has also received his movement order. He will be going to Springhill on Monday, a D-cat. He asks where I'm heading.

'I can't be sure,' I tell him. 'I'm down for the Isle of Wight sometime next week, but I've appealed against the move.'

'Can't blame you. By the way, did you notice how peaceful the workshop was this afternoon?' Ali asks.

'I didn't see any difference from the last time I was there.'

'No, the whole atmosphere changed the moment you walked into the room. The prison officers and even the inmates stop swearing, and a lot more work gets done.'

'I can't believe that.'

'Oh yes,' says Ali, 'they all know you're writing a book and you might mention them by name.'

'Not yours,' I remind him, 'you're still referred to as Ali. You're only the second person who wants their identity kept a secret.'

Once we reach the apex that divides Blocks One and Two, we go our separate ways. I wish him well.

As soon as I'm back in my cell, I grab a McVitie's biscuit and pour out my last mug of water, leaving only a dribble in the bottom of the bottle. I'm about to discover if Del Boy is the man.

I turn on the radio. England are all out for 185. I drown my sorrows in the last cup of water before starting on what I expect to be an extended writing session. I'm fearful of forgetting even a line of William Keane's monologue.

4.30 pm

I turn the radio back on to follow the cricket. Australia are 46 without loss, chasing a total of 185. Shall I continue writing, or be a masochist? I decide to go on listening for a few more minutes. In the next over, Slater is bowled, and by the time the cell door is opened for supper (vegetable pie and beans) Australia are 105 for 7, with only Gilchrist among the recognized batsmen still left at the crease.

7.00 pm

Association. I go in search of Del Boy like a helpless addict desperate for a fix. I find him sitting on his bed, head bowed, looking mournful. He bends down and slowly pulls out from under his bed a large brown-paper bag, and like a conjuror, produces three bottles of Highland Spring and two packets of McVitie's chocolate – I repeat, chocolate – biscuits. He is, unquestionably, the man.

I cuddle him. 'Get off me,' he says pushing me away. 'If anyone saw you doing that, I'd never be able to show my face in the East End again.'

I laugh, thank him, and carry off his spoils to my cell.

I pour myself a mug of water and am munching a chocolate biscuit when there's a knock on the cell door. I look up to see my next-door neighbour, Richard, standing in the doorway. I feel his eyes boring into me. 'The fuckin' *Mirror*,' he says almost in a shout, 'have been round to our fuckin' house and are pestering my fuckin' mum.'

'I'm sorry to hear that,' I say. 'But why are they doing that?'

'Just because I'm in the next fuckin' cell to you,' he says plaintively. I nod my understanding. 'They say you're going to describe me in your fuckin' book as a vicious criminal and they fear for your fuckin' safety. Do you think I'm fuckin' vicious?'

'You've given me no reason to believe so,' I reply.

'Well, now they're threatening my fuckin' mum, telling her that if she doesn't supply a fuckin' photo of me, they'll make it worse.'

'How?' I asked.

'By telling their fuckin' readers what I did.'

'I'm afraid you must phone your mother and explain to her that they'll do that in any case. By the way, what are you in for?'

'Murder,' he replies. 'But it wasn't my fuckin' fault.'

'Why, what happened?'

'I was out drinking with the boys at my fuckin' local, and when we left the fuckin' pub we came face to face with a bunch of fuckin' Aussie backpackers who accused us of stealing their fuckin' wallets. I promise you, Jeff, I'd never seen the fuckin' bastards before in my life.'

'So what happened next?'

'Well, one of 'em had a fuckin' knife, and when my mate punched him, he dropped the fuckin' thing on the pavement. I grabbed it and when another of them came for me, I fuckin' stabbed him. It was only fuckin' self-defence.'

'And he died from one stab?'

'Not exactly.' He hesitates. 'The coroner said there were seven stab wounds, but I was so fuckin' tanked up that I can't remember a fuckin' thing about it.' He pauses. 'So make sure you tell your fuckin' readers that I'm not a vicious criminal.'*

Once Richard returns to his cell, I go back over William Keane's words, before turning to the latest round of letters, still running at over a hundred a day. When I've finished them, I start reading a new book, *The Day after Tomorrow*, recommended by Del Boy – somewhat ironic. It's over seven hundred pages, a length that would normally put me off, but not in my present circumstances. I've only read a few pages, when there's a knock on the cell door. It's Paul (credit-card fraud). They're transferring him tomorrow morning back to the drug-rehab centre in Norfolk, so we may never meet again. He shakes hands as if we were business associates, and then leaves without another word.

---

* *Almost* all of the prisoners have stopped swearing in front of me.

I place my head on a pillow that no longer feels rock-hard, and reflect on the day. I can't help thinking that hurling red balls at Australians is, on balance, preferable to sticking knives into them.

DAY 16   FRIDAY 3 AUGUST 2001

6.07 am

Silent night. Woken by the Alsatians at 6 am. Should have been up in any case. Write for two hours.

8.00 am

Breakfast. Rice Krispies, long-life milk and an orange.

10.00 am

Avoid the workshop. It's not compulsory to do more than three sessions a week. Continue writing.

12 noon

Turn on cricket to hear CMJ telling me that Australia are all out for 190, giving them a lead of only five runs on the first innings. England are still in with a fighting chance.

12.15 pm

Lunch. The rule for lunch and supper – called dinner and tea –

is that you fill in a meal slip the day before and drop it in a plastic box on the ground floor. The menus for the week are posted on a board so you can always select in advance. If you fail to fill in the slip – as I regularly do – you're automatically given 'A'. 'A' is always the vegetarian option, 'B' today is pan-fried fish – that's spent more time swimming in oil than the sea, 'C' is steak and kidney pie – you can't see inside it, so avoid at all costs. Puddings: semolina or an apple. Perhaps this is the time to remind you that each prisoner has £1.27 spent on them for three meals a day. (See pages 192–194.)

When I leave my cell, plastic tray and plastic plate in hand, I join a queue of six prisoners at the hotplate. The next six inmates are not allowed to join the queue until the previous six have been served. This is to avoid a long queue and fighting breaking out over the food. At the right-hand end of the hotplate sits Paul (murder) who checks your name and announces Fossett, C., Pugh, B., Clarke, B., etc. When he ticks my name off, the six men behind the counter, who are all dressed in long white coats, white headgear and wear thin rubber gloves for handling the potatoes or bread, go into a huddle because they know by now there's a fifty–fifty chance I won't want anything and will return to my cell empty-handed.

Tony (marijuana only, escaped to Paris) has recently got into the habit of selecting my meal for me. Today he suggests the steak and kidney pie, slightly underdone, the cauliflower au gratin with duchesse potatoes, or, 'My Lord, you could settle for the creamy vegetable pie.' The server's humour has reached the stage of cutting one potato in quarters and placing a diced carrot on top and then depositing it in the centre of my plastic plate. Mind you, if there's chocolate ice-cream or a lollipop, Del Boy always makes sure I end up with two. I never ate puddings before I went to prison.

WEEK 1   EVENING MENU

CHOICE	MONDAY	DIET
A	VEGETABLE SPRING ROLL	ALL DIETS (VEG)
B	BBQ CHICKEN	ORD|MOS|H
C	MIXED GRILL	ORD
	TUESDAY	
A	TOMATO AND ONION PASTA BAKE	ALL DIETS (VEG)
B	SPICY BEEF RIB	ORD|MOS
C	HAM AND CHEESE PASTA BAKE	ORD|H
	WEDNESDAY	
A	FRIED RICE AND VEGETABLES	ALL DIETS
B	POACHED EGG	ORD|MOS|H|VEG
C	FRIED EGG	ORD|MOS|VEG
	THURSDAY	
A	VEGETABLE PATTIE	ALL DIETS
B	ROAST PORK	ORD|H
C	ROAST BEEF	ORD|MOS|H
	FRIDAY	
A	VEGETABLE SAUSAGE ROLL	ALL DIETS
B	CHICKEN FRIED RICE	ORD|MOS|H
C	BAKED SAUSAGE ROLL	ORD
	SATURDAY	
A	CREAMY VEGETABLE PIE	ALL DIETS
B	COTTAGE PIE	ORD|MOS|H
C	—	
	SUNDAY	
A	SPICY VEGETABLE BAKE	ALL DIETS
B	ROAST BEEF • YORKSHIRE PUDDING	ORD|MOS
C	ROAST TURKEY • STUFFING	ORD|MOS|H

CHOICE	MONDAY	DIET
A	VEGETABLE FINGERS	ALL DIETS
B	FISH CAKES e TOMATO SAUCE	VEG/MOS/ORD
C	BEEF CHOW MEIN	MOS/ORD/H
	TUESDAY	
A	RATATOUILLE e MUSHROOMS	ALL DIETS
B	FISH IN TOMATO e BASIL SAUCE	VEG/MOS/ORD/H
C	LAMB STIFFADO	MOS/ORD
	WEDNESDAY	
A	SPICY VEGETABLE CURRY	ALL DIETS
B	CHICKEN TIKKA MASALA	MOS/ORD/H
C	PORK e APPLE SAUCE	ORD/H
	THURSDAY	
A	SWEET e SOUR VEGETABLES	ALL DIETS
B	CHICKEN STEAK IN BATTER	MOS/ORD/H
C	SWEET AND SOUR PORK	ORD/H
	FRIDAY	
A	VEGETABLE GRILL	ALL DIETS
B	OVEN BAKED FISH	VEG/MOS/ORD/H
C	CORNISH PASTIE	MOS/ORD
	SATURDAY	
A	VEGETABLE CUTLET	ALL DIETS
B	ROAST CHICKEN	MOS/ORD/H
C	—	
	SUNDAY	
A	CURRIED BEANS	ALL DIETS
B	CHEESE AND FRUIT	VEG/MOS/ORD/H
C	CHEESE AND CORNED BEEF	ORD

WEEK 5 LUNCH MENU

CHOICE	MONDAY	DIET
A	VEGETABLE CURRY	ORD|VG|V|MOS|H
B	CHICKEN STEAK	ORD|MOS|H
C	CURRIED LAMB	ORD|MOS
	TUESDAY	
A	SOYA BOLOGNAISE	ORD|VG|V|MOS|H
B	SAUSAGES IN ONION GRAVY	ORD|MOS
C	SPAGHETTI BOLOGNAISE	ORD|MOS|H
	WEDNESDAY	
A	GARLIC AND VEGTABLE STEAK	ORD|VG|V|MOS|H
B	PANE PORK CHOP	ORD
C	POACHED FISH IN PEPPER e TOM	ORD|VG|MOS|H
	THURSDAY	
A	JERK VEGETABLES RICE e COCONUT	ORD|VG|V|MOS|H
B	CHEESE AND ONION FLAN	ORD|VG|MOS
C	JERK CHICKEN RICE e PEAS	ORD|MOS|H
	FRIDAY	
A	CREAMY VEGTABLE PIE	ORD|VG|V|MOS|H
B	PAN FRIED FISH	ORD|VG|MOS
C	STEAK AND KIDNEY PIE	ORD|MOS
	SATURDAY	
A	VEGETABLE BURGER AND ROLL	ORD|VG|V|MOS|H
B	BEEF BURGER AND ROLL	ORD|MOS
C	- - - -	
	SUNDAY	
A	BOMBAY POTATOES	ORD|VG|V|MOS
B	CHEESE AND FRUIT	ORD|VG|MOS|H
C	CORNED BEEF e CHEESE	ORD|MOS

ORD = ORDINARY   MOS = MOSLEM
V = VEGAN   H = HEALTHY OPTION
VG = VEGETARIAN

But today, Tony tells me, there's a special on the menu: shepherd's pie. Now I am a world expert on shepherd's pie, as it has, for the past twenty years, been the main dish at my Christmas party. I've eaten shepherd's pie at the Ivy, the Savoy and even Club 21 in New York, but I have never seen anything like Belmarsh's version of that particular dish. The meat, if it is meat, is glued to the potato, and then deposited on your plastic plate in one large blob, resembling a Turner Prize entry. If submitted, I feel confident it would be shortlisted.

Tony adds, 'I do apologize, my Lord, but we're out of Krug. However, Belmarsh has a rare vintage tap water 2001, with added bromide.' I settle for creamy vegetable pie, an unripe apple and a glass of Highland Spring (49p).

3.18 pm

An officer comes to pick me up and escort me to the Deputy Governor's office. Once again, I feel like an errant schoolboy who is off to visit the headmaster. Once again the headmaster is half my age.

Mr Leader introduces himself and tells me he has some good news and some bad news. He begins by explaining that, because Emma Nicholson wrote to Scotland Yard demanding an inquiry into the collecting and distribution of funds raised for the Kurds, I will have to remain a C-cat prisoner, and will not be reinstated as a D-cat until the police have completed their investigation. On the word of one vengeful woman, I have to suffer further injustice.

The good news, he tells me, is that I will not be going to Camphill on the Isle of Wight, but will be sent to Elmer in Kent, and as soon as my D-cat has been reinstated, I will move on to Springhill. I complain bitterly about the first decision, but quickly come to realize that Mr Leader isn't going to budge. He even accuses me of 'having an attitude' when I attempt to enter a debate on the subject. He wouldn't last very long in the House of Commons.

'It wasn't my fault,' he claims. 'It was the police's decision to instigate an inquiry.'

4.00 pm

Association. David (life imprisonment, possession of a gun) is the only person watching the cricket on television. I pull up a chair and join him. It's raining, so they're showing the highlights of the first two innings. I almost forget my worries, despite the fact that if I was 'on the out', I wouldn't be watching the replay, I would be at the ground, sitting under an umbrella.

6.00 pm

I skip supper and continue writing, which causes a riot, or near riot. I didn't realize that Paul has to tick off every name from the four spurs, and if the ticks don't tally with the number of prisoners, the authorities assume someone has escaped. The truth is that I've only tried to escape supper.

Mr Weedon arrives outside my cell. I look up from my desk and put down my pen.

'You haven't had any supper, Archer,' he says.

'No, I just couldn't face it.'

'That's a reportable offence.'

'What, not eating?' I ask in disbelief.

'Yes, the Governor will want to know if you're on hunger strike.'

'I never thought of that,' I said. 'Will it get me out of here?'

'No, it will get you back on the hospital wing.'

'Anything but that. What do I have to do?'

'Eat something.'

I pick up my plastic plate and go downstairs. Paul and the whole hotplate team are waiting, and greet me with a round of applause with added cries of, 'Good evening, my Lord, your usual table.' I select one boiled potato, have my name ticked off, and return to my cell. The system feels safe again. The rebel has conformed.

7.00 pm

I have a visit from Tony (marijuana only, escaped to France) and he asks if I'd like to join him in his cell on the second floor, as if he were inviting a colleague to pop into his office for a chat about the latest sales figures.

When you enter a prisoner's cell, you immediately gain an impression of the type of person they are. Fletch has books and pamphlets strewn all over the place that will assist new prisoners to get through their first few days. Del Boy has tobacco, phone-cards and food, and only he knows what else under the bed, as he's the spur's 'insider dealer'. Billy's shelves are packed with academic books and files relating to his degree course. Paul has a wall covered in nude pictures, mostly Chinese, and Michael only has photos of his family, mainly of his wife and six-month-old child.

Tony is a mature man, fifty-four, and his shelves are littered with books on quantum mechanics, a lifelong hobby. On his bed is a copy of today's *Times*, which, when he has read it, will be passed on to Billy; reading a paper a day late when you have an eighteen-year sentence is somehow not that important. In a corner of the room is a large stack of old copies of the *Financial*

Times. I already have a feeling Tony's story is going to be a little different.

He tells me that he comes from a middle-class family, had a good upbringing, and a happy childhood. His father was a senior manager with a top life-assurance fund, and his mother a housewife. He attended the local grammar school, where he obtained twelve O-levels, four A-levels and an S-level, and was offered a place at London University, but his father wanted him to be an actuary. Within a year of qualifying he knew that wasn't how he wanted to spend his life, and decided to open a butcher's shop with an old school friend. He married his friend's sister, and they have two children (a daughter who recently took a first-class honours degree at Bristol, and a son who is sixteen and, as I write, boarding at a well-known public school).

By the age of thirty, Tony had become fed up with the hours a butcher has to endure; at the slaughterhouse by three every morning, and then not closing the shop until six at night. He sold out at the age of thirty-five and, having more than enough money, decided to retire. Within weeks he was bored, so he invested in a Jaguar dealership, and proceeded to make a second fortune during the Thatcher years. Once again, he sold out, once again determined to retire, because he was seeing so little of his family, and his wife was threatening to leave him. But it wasn't too long before he needed to find something to occupy his time, so he bought a rundown pub in the East End. Tony thought this would be a distracting hobby until he ended up with fourteen pubs, and a wife whom he hardly saw.

He sold out once more. Having parted from his wife, he found himself a new partner, a woman of thirty-seven who ran her own family business. Tony was forty-five at the time. He moved in with her and quickly discovered that the family business was drugs. The family concentrated on marijuana and wouldn't touch anything hard. There's more than a large enough market out there not to bother with hard drugs, he assures me. Tony made it clear from the start that he had no interest in drugs, and was wealthy enough not to have anything to do with the family business.

The problem of living with this lady, he explained, was that he quickly discovered how incompetently the family firm was being run, so he began to pass on to his partner some simple business maxims. As the months went by he found that he was becoming more and more embroiled, until he ended up as titular MD. The following year they tripled their profits.

'Meat, cars, pubs, Jeffrey,' he said, 'marijuana is no different. For me it was just another business that needed to be run properly. I shouldn't have become involved,' he admits, 'but I was bored, and annoyed by how incompetent her and her family were and to be fair, she was good in bed.'

Now here is the real rub. Tony was sentenced to twelve years for a crime he didn't commit. But he does admit quite openly that they could have nailed him for a similar crime several times over. He was apparently visiting a house he owned to collect the rent from a tenant who had failed to pay a penny for the past six months when the police burst in. They found a fifty-kilo package of marijuana hidden in a cupboard under the stairs, and charged him with being a supplier. He actually knew nothing about that particular stash, and was innocent of the charges laid against him, but guilty of several other similar offences. So he doesn't complain, and accepts his punishment. Very British.

After Tony had served three and a half years, they moved him to Ford Open, a D-cat prison, from where he visited Paris, as already recorded in this diary. He then moved on to Mijas in Spain, and found a job as an engineer, but a friend shafted him – a sort of Ted Francis, he says – 'so I was arrested and spent sixteen months in a Spanish jail, while my extradition papers were being sorted out. They finally sent me back to Belmarsh, where I will remain until I've completed my sentence.' He reminds me that no one has ever escaped from Belmarsh.

'But what happened to the girl?' I ask.

'She got the house, all my money and has never been charged with any offence.' He smiles, and doesn't appear to be bitter about it. 'I can always make money again,' he says. 'That won't be a problem, and I feel sure there will be other women.'

Tony is being considered for parole at the present time, but doesn't get on well with his probation officer. He claims she doesn't appreciate his sense of humour. He warns me to make sure I treat whoever they allocate to my case with respect, because this single individual can be the deciding factor as to whether you should be released or remain locked up in prison.

'So what will you do once you are released?' I ask.

He smiles and extracts a file secreted at the back of his cupboard. 'I'm going to sell agricultural equipment to the Senegalese.' He produces sheet after sheet of financial forecasts on Senegal's agricultural requirements, along with grants the British government will advance to help subsidize that particular industry.

'I wouldn't be surprised if you make a fourth fortune,' I tell him after studying the papers.

'Only women will stop me,' he says. 'I do love them so.'

'Lock-up,' is bellowed from the ground floor. I thank Tony for his company, leave his office, and return to my cell.

8.00 pm

I check over my script for the day and then spend a couple of hours reading my mail. If people go on sending me Bibles and prayer books, I'll be able to open a religious bookshop.

I try to find out the close-of-play cricket score, but have to settle for *Any Questions*. Ken Clarke is very forthright about the iniquity of my sentence, which is brave, remembering he's standing for the leadership of the Tory Party.

10.00 pm

Still no rap music, so for three nights running I can sleep soundly.

DAY 17   SATURDAY 4 AUGUST 2001

6.18 am

Woke several times during the night, not caused by any noise, but simply because I drank too much water yesterday. Cup a Soup (chicken, 22p), Oxo (9p) and a bottle of Highland Spring (69p). Still, I don't have to go that far for the lavatory.

The Alsatians wake me again just after six. Write for two hours.

8.30 am

On a Saturday morning, you are not only allowed to leave your cell, but you also get a cooked breakfast. Egg, beans and chips. I still avoid the chips. Tony selects two fried eggs and the most recently heated beans for me. They taste good.

9.00 am

Association. I seek out Fletch to check over the script I wrote yesterday on drugs. He verifies everything William Keane has told me, and then adds, 'Have you heard of China White?'

'No,' I reply, wondering if it's Wedgwood or Royal Doulton.

'China White was a shipment of pure heroin from the Golden Triangle that turned up in Glasgow a couple of years ago. It was so pure [97 per cent] that fifteen registered addicts died within days of injecting it, and then the stuff began to spread south, killing users right across the country. All prison governors sent out official warnings to inmates, telling them to weaken any dosage of heroin they had recently been supplied with. (See insert.) Come to my cell and I'll show you some literature on the subject.'

Back in his cell, Fletch checks through some papers in a file marked DRUGS. He then hands over several pamphlets and postcards that are given to all suspected drug takers the day they enter prison. It was the first time I'd seen any of this material. They include *The Detox Handbook*, *A User's Guide to Getting off Opiates* (second edition), *The Methadone Handbook* (fifth edition), *Cannabis* (ninth edition), a pamphlet on HIV, Hepatitis B and C, along with six coloured cards: Injecting and Infections (Illustrated):

1) **Cannabis** – marijuana, puff, blow, draw, weed, shit, hash, spliff, tackle, wacky, ganja.
2) **Acid and magic mushrooms** – mushies, 'shrooms (LSD).
3) **Amphetamines** – speed, wizz, uppers, billy, amph, sulphate.
4) **Ecstasy** – E, doves, disco biscuits, echoes, hug drug, burgers, fantasy.
5) **Cocaine** – coke, charlie, snow, C.
6) **Heroin** – smack, gear, brown, horse, junk, scag, jack.

There are several slang names for each drug according to which part of the country you live in. The Misuse of Drugs Act divides illegal drugs into three classes, and provides for maximum penalties of between two and fourteen years.

	Drug type	Maximum penalties
Class A	**Amphetamines (Speed)** *if prepared for injection*	**Possession**: 7 years' prison and/or a fine
	Cocaine and Crack	**Possession with intent to supply, or supply**: life imprisonment and/or a fine
	Ecstasy (and drugs similar to ecstasy)	
	Heroin	
	LSD (Acid)	
	Magic Mushrooms *if prepared for use*	
Class B	**Amphetamines (Speed)** **Cannabis***	**Possession**: 5 years' prison and/or a fine
		Possession with intent to supply, or supply: 14 years' prison and/or a fine
Class C	**Anabolic Steroids** **Benzodiazepines** (e.g. temazepam, flunitrazepam, Valium)	**Possession**: 2 years' prison and/or a fine
		Possession with intent to supply, or supply: 5 years' prison and/or a fine

Fletch tells me that we have our own heroin dealer on the spur, and he knows exactly who his customers are. There are fifty-eight prisoners on our spur and eleven of them are, or have been, on heroin and forty-one of them are currently taking drugs.

I'm about to leave when I see five roses on his window sill. Fletch is obviously a man who likes to have flowers in his room. I look at the little bunch more closely. He makes the petals out

---

* Recently downgraded to Class C.

HMP BELMARSH

GOVERNOR'S NOTICE TO INMATES NO: 64/2001

POSSIBLE BATCH OF CONTAMINATED HEROIN
AT RISK OF CAUSING SEVERE SYSTEMIC SEPSIS
IN INJECTING DRUG USERS

All inmates will be aware that possession, or use, of any controlled drug is an offence against prison discipline. However, any inmate who chooses to ignore this should be aware of possible health risks associated with injecting drugs.

It is possible that parts of a batch of heroin, which may have been responsible for a number of deaths in Scotland, Ireland and various parts of England last year, may be circulating on the drugs market again.

Any inmate who injects drugs is therefore placing himself at extreme risk.

GOVERNOR

of bread, and the raindrop effect on the red petals are grains of sugar. He paints them with a brush made up of hairs that have fallen out of a shaving brush. They are attached to the end of a pencil with the aid of a rubber band. He finally produces the colour by using a wet brush and applying it to the end of a red crayon. He's made six of these bread roses and planted them in a bread roll, as he's not allowed a flower pot because when broken it could be used as a weapon.

'Why won't they let you have a paintbox?' I ask.

'No boxes or tins are allowed in Belmarsh,' he explains, 'because they can also be turned into a weapon and weapons are a massive problem for the screws. They have to allow you a new Bic razor every day, otherwise all the cons would be unshaven. Last month a con glued two Bic razor blades to the end of a toothbrush, caught someone in the shower and left him with a scar across his face that no plastic surgeon will be able to disguise. Whenever you open a can of anything,' Fletch continues, 'you have to tip the contents out onto a plate, and pass the empty can back to an officer, as you could cut someone's throat with the serrated edge of the lid. However,' Fletch adds, 'there are still many other ways a determined prisoner can make himself a weapon.' I don't interrupt his flow.

'For example,' he continues, 'you could hit someone over the head with your steel Thermos flask. You could pour the hot water from your Thermos over another prisoner; you could remove one of the iron struts from under your bed and you'd have a crude knife; I've even seen someone's throat cut with a sharpened phonecard. Fletch picks up his plastic lavatory brush. 'One prisoner quite recently used his razor supply to shave down the handle [nine inches in length] so that he turned his bog brush into a sword, and then in the middle of the night stabbed his cell-mate to death.'

'But that would only ensure that he remained in prison for the rest of his life,' I reminded him.

'He already had a life sentence,' said Fletch without emotion. 'If a prisoner is determined to kill his cell-mate or even another prisoner, it's all too easy, because once you're banged up, the screws can't spend all night checking what's taking place on the other side of the iron door.'

Only two weeks ago I would have been appalled, horrified, disgusted by this matter-of-fact conversation. Am I already becoming anaesthetized, numbed by anything other than the most horrific?

When I leave Fletch's cell, Colin (football hooligan) is waiting to see me. He hands me a copy of his rewritten critique on Frank McCourt's latest book, *'Tis*, as well as a poem that he's written. Colin offers me a banana, not my usual fee for editing, but a fair exchange in the circumstances.

I return to my cell and immediately commit to paper everything Fletch has told me.

12 noon

Lunch. Tony has selected a jacket potato covered in grated cheese. I eat his offering slowly while listening to the cricket on the radio. England have already collapsed, and were all out for 161 in their second innings, leaving Australia to chase a total of 156 to win the match and retain the Ashes. I leave the radio on, kidding myself that if Gough and Caddick make an early breakthrough, we could be in with a chance. Wrong again.

3.00 pm

Exercise. I haven't been out of the building for three days, and decide I must get some fresh air. After being searched, I step out into the yard, and immediately spot the two tearaways who threatened me the last time I took some exercise. They're perched up against the wire at the far end of the yard, skulking. I glance behind to find Billy and Colin are tracking me. Billy adds the helpful comment, 'You need a haircut, Jeffrey.' He's right.

I'm joined on the walk by Peter Fabri, who is all smiles. He's out on Monday, to be reunited with his wife and six-week-old child. As I have been writing about him this week, I check over my facts. 'You were offered a thousand pounds to beat up a witness, in a trial due to be heard at the Bailey in the near future?'

'Even that's changed since I last saw you,' said Peter. 'He's now offering me forty thousand to bump off the witness. He told me that he's made a profit of two hundred thousand on the crime for which he's been charged, so he reckons it's worth forty to have the only witness snuffed out. You know,' says Peter, 'I think if I was in this place for another fortnight, he'd be offering me a hundred grand.'

Home Secretary, I hope you're still paying attention.

Peter remains with me for three more circuits of the yard before he returns to his friends – three other prisoners with sentences of six weeks or less. I continue walking and notice that Billy and Colin have been replaced by Paul and Del Boy. I spot Fletch standing in the far corner. He likes corners, because from such a vantage point he can view his private domain. It becomes clear he has a protection rota working on my behalf, and I feel sure the officers loitering on the far side of the yard are only too aware of what he's up to.

I pass William Keane leaning against the wire fence chatting to his brother. He jumps up and runs across to join me. Paul and Del Boy immediately take a pace forward, and only relax when I put my arm round William's shoulder. After all, I haven't let anyone know which one of those sitting round the perimeter is the cause of problem.

Once again, I use the time to check the facts that William told me in the workshop. He corrects a couple of errors on the price of cocaine and once again explains how pure heroin is diluted/cut before becoming a joey or bags. When he has completed this explanation, I ask him what he intends to do when he's released in twelve weeks' time.

'Salvage,' he says.

'Salvage?' I repeat, thinking this must have something to do with shipping.

'Yes, I'm going to buy old cars, patch them up, see that they get their MOT certificate and then sell them on the estates round here.'

'Can you make an honest living doing that?' I ask.

'I hope so, Jeffrey,' he says, 'because I'm getting too old [thirty-five] for this game. In any case, there's enough of my family costing the government a thousand pounds a week without me adding to the taxpayers' burden. Mind you,' he adds, 'if they had let me out last week I might have ended up murdering someone.' I stop in my tracks and Paul and Del Boy almost collide into the back of me. 'My brother's just told me' – he points to the other side of the yard where a tall, dark-haired young man is leaning up against the fence – 'that my sister Brinie was kidnapped last week and repeatedly raped, and as most of the family are in jail, there's not a lot we can do about it.' I'm speechless. 'The bastard's been arrested, so we must hope that the judge gets it right this time.' He pauses. 'But for his sake let's hope he doesn't end up in the same prison as one of my brothers. Mind you,' he adds, 'don't bet on that, because the odds are quite short.'

As we turn the corner, he points up to a tower block in the distance. 'That's where another of my brothers, Patrick, fell to his death.' (Have you noticed that Mrs Keane has named all her sons after saints or kings?) 'You'll remember, that was the occasion when the whole family attended his funeral along with half the Metropolitan Police.' He pauses. 'They're now saying he might have been pushed. I'll find out more as soon as I get out of here, and if he was...' What hope has this man of remaining on the outside? I ask myself. I found out a few months later when I met up with yet another brother.*

When William slips off to rejoin his brother, I notice that Del Boy and Paul have been replaced by Tony and David. David (fifty-five, in possession of a gun) is overweight, out of shape and finding it difficult to keep up with me. The next person to join me is a young, bright, full-of-life West Indian, whose story I will not repeat, as it is the mirror image of Peter Fabri's. He too has no intention of even going through an amber light once they release him from Belmarsh. However, he admits that he's learnt a lot more about crime than he knew before he came into prison. He's also been introduced to drugs in the cell he shares with two other inmates.

'I'm clean, man,' he says rubbing his hands together. 'But one of the guys in my cell who's due out next week has tried heroin for the first time. He's hooked now, man, I tell you he's hooked.'

Are you still paying attention, Home Secretary?

I pass the tearaways, who haven't moved an inch for the past forty minutes and have to satisfy themselves with malevolent

---

* This sentence was added while I was editing Volume One, and had finally been transferred to a D-cat. As of today, 1 October 2002, William Keane is still 'on the out'.

stares. I feel confident that they aren't going to risk anything this time.

At four o'clock, we're called back in block by block. Several prisoners who are leaving next week including Peter (offered forty thousand to murder a witness), Denzil (come and see me when I'm a star), and Liam (do I need a barrister or should I represent myself?) come across to shake hands and wish me luck. I pray that they never see the inside of Belmarsh again.

4.00 pm

When I arrive back in my cell there's another stack of letters waiting for me on my bed, three stacks to be accurate. I start reading. It's turned out to be most helpful that the censor has to open every one. I'm particularly touched by a letter Freddie Forsyth sent to the *Daily Telegraph* about the length of my sentence, and the money I've raised for charity. The editor did not publish it.

5.49 pm

Last call for supper. Spur one is always let out first and called back last, because most of the inmates are lifers who will spend more time inside than anyone else on the block. It's prison logic and works because the turnover on the other three spurs is between 10 per cent and 20 per cent a week, so no one thinks of complaining.

I stroll down to the hotplate, but only so that my name can be ticked off, pick up a Thermos of hot water and return to my cell. I make myself a Cup a Soup (tomato, 22p) and eat a Mars Bar (31p) and a prison apple, as I continue to read today's letters.

DAY 17

6.30 pm

I pick up Colin's critique of Frank McCourt's *'Tis*. The improvement is marked since I read his first effort. He has now sorted out how much of the story he should reveal before he offers his critical opinion. This is obviously a man who once you tell him something is able to respond immediately. I then turn my attention to his poem.

Education Belmarsh

Open the labyrinths of time
blow out the cobwebs
and past life of crime
full of knowledge held within
the mind is truly a wonderful thing

It can be educated, it can be evolved
without education
can the problems be solved?

While locked away, there is plenty to see
they entrap the body
but your mind is still free
to wander the universe
and grow like a tree

So go to the library
and pick up a book
watch your mind grow
while other cons look

It's not down to them
to make you move
so go ahead read
and your mind will improve

Colin Kitto, May 2001
House Block 1, HMP Belmarsh

This poem reveals a lot about the man, where he's going, and where he's come from. I feel sure that before he completes his sentence, he will have that degree from Ruskin College. And don't forget, this is a man who couldn't read or write before he came into prison.

There is a polite knock on the door and I look up to see one of the officers peering through my little oblong window. He asks if I would be willing to sign autographs for his two daughters, Joanna and Stephanie. 'They both enjoy your books,' he explains, before adding, 'though I must admit I've never read one.'

He doesn't unlock the cell door, just pushes two pieces of paper underneath. This puzzles me. I later learn that an officer cannot unlock a cell door if he is not on duty. Once he has retrieved them, he adds, 'I'll be off for the first part of next week, so if I don't see you again, good luck with your appeal.'

7.30 pm

I begin reading a book of short stories that had been left on a table by the TV on the ground floor. It's titled *The Fallen* and the author, John MacKenna, is someone I've not read before. He's no storyteller, as so often the Irish are, but oh, don't I wish I could write as lyrically as he does.

9.50 pm

I finish reading John MacKenna in one sitting (on the end of the bed) – what assured, confident prose, with an intimate feel for his countrymen and his country. I conclude that God gave the Irish the gift of language and threw in some potatoes as an afterthought.

DAY 18   SUNDAY 5 AUGUST 2001

6.00 am

Another good night's sleep.

Yesterday I wrote for six hours, three sessions of two, read for three – including my letters – and slept for eight. Out there where you are, five hours' sleep was always enough. In truth, the writing is an attempt to fill the day and night with nonstop activity. I feel sorry for the prisoners who have to occupy those same hours and cannot read or write.

8.00 am

Breakfast. A treat. Egg and beans on toast, two mornings in a row. I don't grumble. I've always liked egg and beans.

9.30 am

I hear the officer on duty holler up from his desk, 'RCs.'

I press the buzzer which switches on a red light outside my door – known as room service – to indicate that I wish to attend chapel. No one comes to unlock the door. When they yell a second time, I press the buzzer again, but still no one responds.

After they call a third time, I start banging on my door, but to no avail. Although I am not a Roman Catholic, after William Keane's recommendation I would have liked to hear Father Kevin preach.

10.03 am

Mr Cousins finally appears to explain that as I am not a Roman Catholic, the officer on duty assumed my name had been put on the wrong list, and transferred me back to C of E. I curse under my breath as I don't want to be put on report. A curse for me is damn or blast.

'You can always go next week,' he says. 'Just be sure you give us enough notice.'

'I was rather hoping that I won't be with you next week,' I tell him.

He smiles. I can see he accepts that his colleague has made a mistake, so I decide this might be a good opportunity to ask about the drug problem as seen from the other side of the iron barrier. To my surprise Mr Cousins is frank – almost enthusiastic – about passing on his views.

Mr Cousins doesn't try to pretend that there isn't a drug problem in prisons. Only a fool would. He also admits that because of the casual way officers have to conduct their searches, it's not that difficult to transfer drugs from spur to spur, block to block and even across a table during family visits.

'Not many officers,' he tells me, 'would relish the idea of having to use rubber gloves to search up prisoners' backsides three or four times a day. And even if we did go to that extreme, the inmates would simply swallow the drugs, which would only cause even more problems. But,' he continues, 'we still do everything in our power to prevent and cure, and we've even had a few successes.' He pauses. 'But not that many.'

When a prisoner enters Belmarsh he has an MDT. This takes the form of a urine sample which is all very well until it comes to heroin, a substance that can be flushed through the body within twenty-four hours. Most other drugs leave some signs in the blood or urine for at least four weeks. On the day they enter prison, 70 per cent of inmates show positive signs of being on drugs, and even with the twenty-four-hour proviso, 20 per cent indicate of heroin. If Mr Cousins had revealed these figures to me only three weeks ago, he would have left me staggered by the enormity of the problem. Already I have come to accept such revelations as part of everyday prison life.

'Our biggest success rate,' continues Mr Cousins, 'is among those prisoners coming up for parole, because towards the end of their sentence, they have to report regularly to the Voluntary Drug Testing Centre – there's one in every prison – to prove they are no longer dependent on drugs, which will be entered on their report, and can play a part in shortening their sentence. What we don't know,' he adds, 'is how many of them go straight back on drugs the moment they're released. But in recent years we've taken a more positive step to stamp out the problem.

'In 1994 we set up a Dedicated Search Team, known as the ghost-busters, who can move in at any time without warning and search individual cells, even whole spurs or blocks. This team of officers was specifically formed following the IRA escape from Whitemoor Prison in '93, but after all the terrorists were sent back to Ulster following the Good Friday Agreement, the unit switched their concentration from terrorism to the misuse of illegal substances. They've had remarkable success in uncovering large amounts of drugs and charging offenders. But,' he reflects, 'I have to admit the percentage of drug takers still hasn't fallen, and I speak as someone who was once a member of the DST. Mind you,' he adds, 'it's just possible that standing still is in itself an achievement.'

I hear the first bellow from downstairs for C of E, and thank Mr Cousins for his tutorial and his candour.

10.30 am

I report to the middle floor and join those prisoners who wish to attend the morning service. We line up and are put through the usual search before being escorted to the chapel. Malcolm (Salvation Army officer) is surprised to see me, as I had told him yesterday that I intended to go and hear Father Kevin preach. Before I take my seat in the second row, I give him the précised version of how I ended up back in his flock.

No backing group this week, just taped music, which makes Malcolm's job all the more difficult, especially when it comes to stopping the chattering in the back six rows. My eyes settle on a couple of Lebanese drug dealers sitting in the far corner at the back. They are deep in conversation. I know that they're from different spurs, so they obviously use this weekly get together to exchange information on their clients. Every time I turn to observe them, their heads are bowed, but not in prayer.

The sermon this week is taken from Luke. It's the one about the ninety-nine sheep who are safely locked up in the pen while the shepherd goes off in search of the one that's strayed. Malcolm faces a congregation of over two hundred that have strayed, and most of them have absolutely no intention of returning to the pen.

But he somehow battles on, working assiduously on the first six rows, with whom he is having some success. Towards the end of the service his wife reads a lesson, and after the blessing,

DAY 18

Malcolm asks his congregation if they would like to come forward and sign the pledge. At least forty prisoners rise from their places and begin to walk forward. They are individually blessed before signing the register.

They look to me like the same forty who offered themselves up for salvation last week, but I am still in no doubt that Malcolm and his wife are performing a worthwhile mission.

12 noon

Lunch. I settle for more beans on toast, an apple and a mug of water. I suppose I should have stated the obvious at some point, namely that alcohol is forbidden, which is no great loss to me as I rarely drink more than a glass of red wine in the evening.

4.00 pm

Association. I run downstairs, phonecard in hand, thirteen units left for Mary. A long queue has already formed behind the two payphones. One of the disadvantages of living on the top floor.

I turn my attention to the large TV in the middle of the room. Several prisoners are watching the Sunday afternoon film with Tom Hanks and Geena Davis. It's the story of a women's baseball team set up in 1942 when, because of the outbreak of the Second World War, the men's teams had to be disbanded.

I turn my head every few moments but the queue doesn't seem to diminish, so I go on watching the film. Several prisoners join me during the next half-hour.

Del Boy (murder) to tell me he's somehow purloined a copy of the weekly menu for my diary.

Fletch (murder) wants to come to my cell at six and read something to me. I ask if he could make it seven, as I'll still be

218

writing at six. 'Suits me,' he says, 'I'm not going anywhere.' Prison humour.

Tony (marijauna only, escaped to Paris) then leans across and asks if the identification of one of his girlfriends could be removed from yesterday's script. I agree and make a note of her name.

I spot Billy (murder) and recommend the book of short stories by John MacKenna, but he walks on past me without a word. I suppose by now I shouldn't be surprised by anything.

Dennis (GBH, large bag of toiletries) taps me on the shoulder. He starts to tell me about the visit of his son on his first birthday, and how he can't wait to get out and be with his wife and children. Join the club.

Miah (murder) who's the spur hair cutter – known, not surprisingly, as Sweeny Todd – says he can fit me in at seven tomorrow evening. I thank him, explaining that I must have my hair cut before Mary and the boys come to visit me on Thursday. When I glance round, the queue for the phone is down to three. I leave Mr Hanks and Ms Davis and take my place at the back.

Just as I reach the front, another prisoner barges in front of me. As he's a double murderer and his right hand has HATE tattooed on his four fingers, I decide not to mention that I thought I was next in line. Ten minutes later he slams down the phone and walks away effing and blinding. I slowly dial the Cambridge number to be reminded that I only have thirteen units left on my card. Mary answers. She sounds cheerful and is full of news. The trip to Dresden went well, and while she was abroad she felt her life was getting back to normal. Perhaps because the German tabloids aren't quite that obsessed with my incarceration. William accompanied her, and was a tower of strength, while James stayed behind to manage the shop.

Ten units left.

Mary tells me that following Emma Nicholson's letter the police are hinting that they may not even carry out an inquiry. I explain that despite this I've been reassigned to C-cat status, and would like my D-cat back as quickly as possible. She assures me that Ramona and James are working on it.

Seven units left.

I tell her how many letters I have been receiving every day, and she counters by saying that she's getting so many at home and in London that there just aren't enough hours to answer them all. She's designed an all-purpose reply so that she can get on with her own work.

Five units left.

Mary adds that not only are my friends remaining constant, but she's had a dozen offers to join them on their yachts or in their holiday homes, and one even on safari. I've always known we had foul-weather friends, but both of us have been touched by the public's overwhelming support.

Three units left.

I let her know that I've already written over forty thousand words of the diary, but can't be sure what my regular readers will make of it. Mary says she's looking forward to reading an early draft, and will give me a candid view. She is incapable of doing anything else.

One unit left.

We begin our goodbyes, and she reminds me I will be seeing her and the boys on Thursday, something to look forward to.

'Do you know how much I . . .'

All units used up. I hear a click, and the phone goes dead.

As I walk away, I hear the words 'Lock-up' bellowed out from just behind me. As reliable as Big Ben, if not as melodious. It has to be five o'clock.

6.05 pm

Supper. I go down to the hotplate and have my name ticked off by Paul – prisoners do a seven-day week with no holidays or bank holidays – and pick up a Thermos flask of hot water and a chocolate ice cream. Back in my cell I make a Cup a Soup (mushroom, 22p), eat another Mars Bar (31p), and enjoy a chocolate ice-cream (prison rations).

7.00 pm

I'm washing my plastic plate in the basin when there's a knock on the door. The cell door is pulled open by an officer to reveal the massive frame of Fletch standing in the doorway. I had quite forgotten he was coming to read something to me.

I smile. 'Welcome,' I say, like the spider to the fly. The first thing I notice is that he's clutching a small green notebook, not unlike the type we used to write our essays in at school. After a brief chat about which prison I'm likely to be sent to, and his opinion of Mr Leader, the Deputy Governor, he turns to the real purpose of his visit.

'I wonder if I might be allowed to read something to you?' he asks.

'Of course,' I reply, not sure if it's to be an essay, a poem, or even the first chapter of a novel. I settle on the bed while Fletch sits in the plastic chair (prisoners are only allowed one chair per cell). He places the little lined book on my desk, opens it at the first page, and begins to read.

If I had the descriptive powers of Greene and the narrative drive of Hemingway, I still could not do justice to the emotions I went through during the next twenty minutes; revulsion, anger, sympathy, incredulity, and finally inadequacy. Fletch turns another page, tears welling up in his eyes, as he forces himself to resurrect the demons of his past. By the time he comes to the last page, this giant of a man is a quivering wreck, and of all the emotions I can summon up to express my true feelings, anger prevails. When Fletch closes the little green book, we both remain silent for some time.

Once I'm calm enough to speak, I thank him for the confidence he has shown in allowing me to share such a terrible secret.

'I've never allowed anyone in Belmarsh to read this,' he says, tapping the little green book. 'But perhaps now you can appreciate why I won't be appealing against my sentence. I don't need the whole world to know what I've been through,' he adds in a whisper, 'so it will go with me to my grave.' I nod my understanding and promise to keep his confidence.

10.00 pm

I can't sleep. What Fletch has read to me could not have been made up. It's so dreadful that it has to be true. I sleep for a few minutes and then wake again. Fletch has tried to put the past behind him by devoting his time and energy to being a Listener, helping others, by sharing his room with a bullied prisoner, a drug addict, or someone likely to be a victim of sexual abuse.

I fall asleep. I wake again. It's pitch black outside my little cell window and I begin to feel that Fletch could give an even greater service if his story were more widely known, and the truth exposed. Then people like me who have led such naive and sheltered lives could surely have the blinkers lifted from their eyes.

I decide as soon as they let me out of my cell, that I will tell him that I've changed my mind. I'm going to suggest that he could do far more good by revealing what actually happened to him than by remaining silent. In all, I think I've woken five or six times during the night, my thoughts always returning to Fletch. But one comment he made above all others burns in my mind, *Fifty per cent of prisoners in Belmarsh can tell you variations of the same story. Jeffrey, my case is not unique.*

I decide I must use whatever persuasive powers I possess to get him to agree to publish, without reservation, everything in that little green book.

DAY 19　　　MONDAY 6 AUGUST 2001

5.17 am

I've spent a sleepless night. I rise early and write for two hours.
When I've finished, I pace around my cell, aware that if only I
had held onto Fletch's little green notebook I could have spent
the time considering his words in greater detail.

8.00 am

I know I've eaten a bowl of Corn Pops from my Variety pack,
because I can see the little empty box in the waste-paper bin,
but I can't remember when. I go on pacing.

9.00 am

An officer opens the cell door. I rush down to the ground floor,
only to discover that Fletch is always let out at eight so that he
can go straight to the workshops and have everything set up
and ready before the other prisoners arrive. Because of the
length of his sentence, it's a real job for him. He's the works
manager, and can earn up to forty pounds a week. I could
go along to the workshops, but with seventy or eighty other

prisoners hanging around, I wouldn't be able to hold a private conversation with him. Tony tells me Fletch will be back for dinner at twelve, when he'll have an hour off before returning to the workshops at one. I'll have to wait.

When I return to my cell, I find a letter has been pushed under my door. It's from Billy Little (murder). He apologizes for being offhand with me during Association the previous evening. August is always a bad month for him, he explains, and he's not very good company for a number of reasons:

I last saw my son in August 1998, my favourite gran died in August, the heinous act of murder that I committed took place on August 22, 1998. As you can imagine, I have a lot on my mind.

I can't begin to imagine, which I admit when I reply to his letter. He continues . . .

During this period, I tend to spend a long time inside myself. This could give an impression to those who don't know me of being ignorant and unapproachable. For this I apologise.

By this time tomorrow, you'll be sunning it up by the pool, or that's how Springhill will feel in comparison to Hellmarsh. In a way, you've been lucky to have spent only a short period here, a period in which you've brought the normal inertia of prison to life.

Over the last three weeks you will have felt the resentment of other prisoners who feel strongly that equality should be practised even in prisons. You no doubt recall the Gilbert and Sullivan quote from *The Gondoliers* – when everybody is some- body, then nobody is anybody.

I think what I'm trying to say is that your status, friend- liness and willingness to help and advise others has not gone unnoticed by those who are destined to spend a great deal longer incarcerated.

For this I thank you, and for your inspiration to press me to think more seriously about my writing. I would like to take you up on your offer to keep in touch, and in particular to check over my first novel.

I'll be resident here for another month or two, or three, before they move me onto a first stage lifer main centre [*Billy has been at Belmarsh for two years and seven months*] I'll let you know my address once I've settled. My number is at the bottom of this letter.

You are Primus Inter Pares

Yours,

Billy (BX7974)

I sit down at my table and reply immediately.

12 noon

When Fletch arrives back from the workshops, he finds me waiting by his cell door. He steps inside and invites me to join him.* I ask if I might be allowed to borrow his notebook so that I can consider more carefully the piece he read to me the previous evening. He hesitates for a moment, then goes to a shelf above his bed, burrows around and extracts the little green notebook. He hands it over without comment.

I grab an apple for lunch and return to my cell. Reading Fletch's story is no less painful. I go over it three times before pacing up and down. My problem will be getting him to agree to publish his words in this diary.

------

* You never enter someone else's cell unless invited to do so.

3.37 pm

Mr Bentley opens my cell door to let me know that the Deputy Governor wishes to see me. As I am escorted to Mr Leader's office, I can only wonder what bad news he will have to impart this time. Am I to be sent to Parkhurst or Brixton, or have they settled on Dartmoor? When the Deputy Governor's door is opened, I am greeted with a warm smile. Mr Leader's demeanour and manner are completely different from our last meeting. He is welcoming and friendly, which leads me to hope that he is the bearer of better news.

He tells me that he has just heard from the Home Office that I will not be going to Camphill on the Isle of Wight or Elmer in Kent, but Wayland. I frown. I've never heard of Wayland.

'It's in Norfolk,' he tells me. 'C-cat and very relaxed. I've already spoken to the Governor,' he adds, 'and only one other member of my staff is aware of your destination.' I take this as a broad hint that it might be wise not to tell anyone else on the spur of my destination, unless I want to be accompanied throughout the entire journey by the national press. I nod and realize why he has taken the unusual step of seeing me alone. I'm about to ask him a question, when he answers it.

'We plan to move you on Thursday.'

Only three more days at Hellmarsh, is my first reaction, and, after asking him several more questions, I thank him and return to my cell unescorted. I spend the next hour considering every word Mr Leader has said. I recall asking him which he would rather be going to, Wayland or the Isle of Wight. 'Wayland,' he'd replied without hesitation.

In prison it's necessary to fight each battle day by day if you're eventually going to win the war. First it was getting off the medical centre and onto Block Three. Then was escaping

DAY 19

Block Three (Beirut) and being moved to Block One to live among a more mature group of prisoners. Next was being transferred from Belmarsh to a C-cat prison. Now I shall be pressing to regain my D-cat status, so that I can leave Wayland as quickly as possible for an open prison. But that's tomorrow's battle. Several prisoners have 'Take each day as it comes' scrawled on their walls.

4.00 pm

I try to write, but so much has already happened today that I find it hard to concentrate. I munch a bar of Cadbury's Fruit and Nut (32p), and drink a mug of Evian (49p) topped up with Robinson's blackcurrant juice (97p).

6.00 pm

Supper. I catch Fletch in the queue for the hotplate, and he agrees to join me in my cell at seven. 'Miah [murder] is cutting my hair at seven,' I tell him, 'so could we make it seven fifteen? I can't afford to miss the appointment, as I'm still hoping for a visit from my wife on Thursday.'

7.00 pm

Association. I sit patiently in a chair on number 2 landing waiting for Miah. He doesn't turn up on time to cut my hair, so I return to my cell and wait for Fletch. He does arrive on time and takes a seat on the end of the bed. He doesn't bother with any preamble.

'You can include my piece in your book if you want to,' he says, 'and if you do, let's hope it does some good.'

I tell him that if a national newspaper serializes the diary, then his words will be read by millions of people, and the politicians will have to finally stop pretending that it isn't happening or they will simply be guilty by association.

We begin to go through the script line by line, filling in details such as names, times and places so that the casual reader can properly follow the sequence of events. Tony (marijuana only) joins us a few minutes later. It turns out that he's the only other person to have read the piece, and it also becomes clear that it was on his advice that Fletch decided not only to write about his experiences, but to allow a wider audience to read them.

There's a knock on the door. It's Miah (murder). He apologizes about missing his appointment to cut my hair, but he's only just finished his spell on the hotplate. He explains that he can't fit me in tomorrow, because of his work schedule, but he could cut my hair during Association on Wednesday. I warn him that if he fails to keep the appointment on Wednesday, I'll kill him, as my wife is coming to visit me on Thursday and I must look my best. Miah laughs, bows and leaves us. *I'll kill him.* I said it without thinking, and to a convicted murderer. Miah is 5ft 4in, and I doubt if he weighs ten stone; the man he murdered was 6ft 2in and weighed 220 pounds. Strange world I'm living in.

Fletch, Tony and I continue to go over the script, and when we've completed the task, Fletch stands up and shakes me by the hand to show the deal has been agreed.

8.00 pm

For the next two hours, I transcribe out Fletch's words, adding to the script only when he has given me specific details, background or names. By the time I've completed the last sentence, I'm even more angry than I was when he read the piece to me last night.

10.00 pm

I lie awake in my thin, hard prison bed, my head resting on my thinner, harder prison pillow, and wonder how decent normal people will react to Fletch's story. For here is a man of whom any one of us might say, there but for the grace of God go I.

These are the words of the prisoner known as Fletch (murder, life imprisonment, minimum sentence twenty-two years).

My name is . . .* I am thirty-eight years old and serving a life sentence for a murder I did not commit, but I only wish I had.

My whole life has been a fuck-up from the start. I was born in Morriston in Wales and although I loved my family, I have only had six real relationships in my life, or as real as I felt they could be. The sort of relationship you want to rush home to, and regret leaving in the morning when you return to work.

I met my wife when I was seventeen, and even today would happily die for her. We had a twenty-year relationship, though both of us had other lovers during that time. Of the six relationships I've had, two have been with men, which is where the complication begins. Because of years of sexual abuse I suffered during my childhood, I have never really enjoyed sex, whether it be with a man or a woman.

Even today, I detest sexual contact and accept that it is what has caused the break-up of my relationships. I was always able to perform, and perform it was, but in truth it was nothing more than a chore, and I gained no gratification from it.

---

*I presented Fletch's original script to my publisher in full; names and places have been necessarily omitted from the final text.

I never felt able to tell my wife the truth about my past, despite the twenty years we'd shared together. It's so easy to claim you've been abused, and shift the blame onto someone else. It's so easy to claim you couldn't prevent it, and it's also virtually impossible to prove it.

The truth is that I had no idea that what I was experiencing wasn't the norm. Wasn't every child going through this? My childhood ended at the age of nine when I was sent to a home.

Overnight I became a plaything for those who were employed to care for me, those in power. They even managed to secure a place of safety order from a court so I couldn't be moved and *they* could carry on abusing me.

During the 1970s corporal punishment was common in children's homes. For some of the staff it was simply the way they got their kicks. First they caned little boys until they screamed, and then they buggered us until we were senseless; not until then did they stop. Nine other children from that home can confirm this statement; two are married with children of their own, two are gay, five are in jail.

Two of the five in jail are serving life sentences for murder.

After a time, the abuse becomes a form of love and affection, because if you didn't want to be caned, or belted with a strap, you give in and quickly accept the alternative, sexual abuse. By the age of twelve, I knew more about perversion and violence than any one of you reading this have ever read about, or even seen in films, let alone experienced.

By the age of twelve, I had been abused by the staff at my home in —, local social workers, care staff and a probation officer. All of these professions attract paedophiles, and although they are in the minority (20%), they are well aware of each other, and they network together, and most frightening of all, they protect each other.

I know a child who was articulate enough by the age of fourteen to tell the authorities what he was being put through, so they just moved him around the country from home to home before anyone could begin an investigation, while other paedophiles carried on abusing him.

At the age of thirteen I ran away and made my way to ——. When I reached ——, I began sleeping rough in ——. It was there that I first met a man called *****, who offered me somewhere to sleep. That night he got me drunk, not too difficult when you're only thirteen. He raped me, and after that began renting me out to like-minded men. Whenever you read in the tabloid press about rent boys for sale, don't assume that they do it by choice, or even that they're paid. They are often locked up, and controlled like any other prostitute, and have little or no say in what happens to their life.

***** controlled me for about six months, bringing to the flat judges, schoolmasters, police officers, politicians and other upstanding citizens who are the back-bone of our country (I can tell you of birthmarks, wounds and peculiarities for almost every one of these men).

One night in the West End when I was still thirteen, I was arrested by the police while ***** was trying to sell me to a customer. I was collected from the nick by a social worker, who took me to a children's home in ——. The home was run by a magistrate, ******. For the next fourteen days, [he] buggered me night and day before issuing a court order that I should be returned to [my original children's home], where it was back to caning and systematic abuse.

After a couple of months, I was transferred to ——, a hospital for emotionally disturbed children. Once again, the staff abused me and this time they had a more effective weapon than caning. They threatened to apply EST, electric shock treatment should I try to resist. I ran away again, returning to ——, and have lived there ever since. I was only fourteen at the time, and ***** soon caught up with me. This time he installed me in the flat of a friend where seven or eight men would bugger me on a daily basis. One or two liked to whip me with a belt, while others punched me, this could be before, during or after having sex. When they eventually stopped, they occasionally left a small present (money or gift) on my pillow. This wasn't much use, because I never got out of the flat, unless I was accompanied by *****.

By the age of fifteen, I was sniffing glue, regularly getting drunk, and having sex with countless men. But it didn't hurt any more. I felt nothing, it was all just part of my daily life.

This life, if that's what you can call it, continued for another four years, during which time I was photographed for porn magazines, and appeared in porn films.

By the age of eighteen, I no longer served any purpose for these men, so I was thrown out onto the street and left to fend for myself. That was when I committed my first crime. Burglary of a department store, Lillywhites. I was arrested and sent to Borstal for six months. When I was released, I continued with a life of crime, I wasn't exactly trained for anything else.

By now I was six foot one and weighed 190 pounds, so didn't find it difficult to get a job in security, which is so often on the fringes of crime.

In 1980, at the age of eighteen, I met my future wife, who had no idea what my real job was, or that for twelve years I had been sexually abused. During the next five years, we had two sons, and twelve years later in 1997, we decided to get married.

I was already earning a good living as a criminal, and everything went well until I was arrested in 1997 for DSS fraud. I had been making false claims in several names for several years, to the tune of £2.8 million, for which I received a three year sentence, which caused my marriage to be put off.

During my time in jail, I began by letter and telephone, to let my wife know that I had for sometime been involved in a life of crime. But it wasn't until I was released that I revealed to her any details of the sexual abuse I had been put through. Her reaction was immediate and hostile. She was disgusted, and reviled, and said she couldn't understand why I hadn't reported these men to the authorities. What authorities were there for me to report to? 'I was only nine years old when it all began. After all it was the authorities who were buggering me,' I told her, 'and by the age of eighteen, when I was no longer of any use to them, they threw me out onto the streets.'

She couldn't come to terms with it. So I was rejected once again, and this time it was by someone I cared for, which made it far worse. She described me as a filthy person, who allowed dirty old men to rape me, because I wanted love and affection. There was no way I could begin to make her understand.

By being open and honest, I had lost the one person I truly loved. My life had been ruined by these evil men, and now they had even robbed me of my wife and two children.

All I now wanted was to kill the five monsters who were responsible, and then die in the hands of the police.

There were five paedophiles who had taken away my life, so I planned to take away theirs. I quickly discovered that two of them had already died, so there were only three left for me to deal with. Their names were ***, **** and *****.

I carefully planned how I would kill them, and then later die in the hands of the police.

I drove down to —and kidnapped *** and brought him back to —, leaving him at my flat with three friends, who agreed to guard him while I returned to the coast to pick up *****. I then planned to go onto — and collect **** and bring them both back to —.

I arrived back in — at one-thirty in the afternoon, when *****'s next door neighbour told me that I had just missed him. I phoned — to warn them that I would be late, because I couldn't risk grabbing him in broad daylight. It was then that they told me the news. They had already killed ***.

I was enraged. I've always been a cold person emotionally, but I cried on the journey back to London, because I had wanted to kill *** myself. I had needed to cleanse myself of these three evil men, and all I had now was a dead body on my hands and three terrified associates.

I drove back to —, breaking the speed limit most of the way. On arrival, I cleaned all the finger-prints from my flat and told the others that I would deal with ***** and **** in my own way. That was when the police burst in; twenty-four armed officers pinned the three of us to the ground, handcuffed and arrested me.

I discovered later that ***** had already phoned the police and told them he feared for his life. I gave my solicitor all the details, and he said that because I was in __ at the time of ***'s death, they wouldn't charge me with murder, but they could charge me with conspiracy to murder. They charged me with murder, and I was sentenced to a minimum of twenty-two years.

Yes, I am doing a twenty-two year sentence for a crime I didn't commit. I only wish I had, and I also wish I had killed **** and ***** at the same time.

I am now a Listener at Belmarsh and feel useful for the first time in my life. I know I've saved one life, and hopefully helped many others.

My demons still haunt me, of course they do, but I somehow keep them at bay. I won't complete my twenty-two year sentence, but I will choose the time and manner of my death.*

It's only shame that prevents me from contacting anyone I know. A feeling of worthlessness, a dirty little rent boy that allowed older men to use, beat and abuse him, because he needed to be loved, and no longer cared what happened to

---

* Fletch subsequently attempted to commit suicide on 7 January 2002.

him. How can I ever expect my wife, my children, or my family to understand?

I hope by telling this story, I may save someone else from the horror I've been put through, so that that person will never be visited by the same demons, and worse, will not end up in jail on a charge of murder.

11.23 pm

I go to bed asking myself should the man known as Fletch have to spend the rest of his life in jail? If the answer is yes, don't we perhaps have some responsibility to the next generation, to ensure that there aren't other children whose lives will end by the age of nine?

DAY 20   TUESDAY 7 AUGUST 2001

6.16 am

I have a better night's sleep. Perhaps Fletch's allowing his story
to be committed to paper has helped. I write for two hours.

8.00 am

Breakfast. Frosties and the last dribble from the second carton of
long-life milk. Not quite enough left to soak my cereal. Canteen
provisions due in today, and as I'm leaving on Thursday I will be
able to repay all my bubbles: Del Boy (water and biscuits), Tony
(Mars Bar), and Colin (stamps, twelve first-class).

10.00 am

Association. I am strolling around the ground floor, when I
notice that one of the prisoners, Joseph (murder), is playing pool.
He's by far the best player on the spur and occasionally clears
the table. This morning he's missing simple shots that even I
would sink. I lean against the wall and watch him more carefully.
He has that distant look on his face, so common among lifers.

When the match is over and the cues have been passed on

to waiting inmates, I comment on his standard of play. I think
the word I select is rubbish.

'I've got something on my mind, Jeff,' he says, still distant.

'Anything I can help with?' I ask.

'No thanks, it's a family matter.'

11.00 am

I see that my name is chalked up on the board for a legal visit
from my solicitor, Tony Morton-Hooper.

Over the years I have found that professional relationships
fall into two categories. The ones that remain professional,
and the ones when you become friends. Tony falls firmly
into the second category. We have a mutual love of athletics
– he has represented many track stars over the years – and
despite a considerable age difference, we relax in each other's
company.

We meet up in one of those small rooms where I come in
from one side and am locked in, and moments later he enters by
a door on the opposite side, and is also locked in. The first thing
I notice is that Tony is wearing a thick yellow rubber band
around his wrist; it will allow him to eventually escape, but for
the next hour he is also incarcerated.

Tony begins by telling me that Wayland Prison is certain to
be a far more relaxed regime than Belmarsh, and as good a place
as any to be until I am reinstated as a Category D prisoner. I ask
Tony what the latest is on that subject.

'It's all good news,' he tells me. 'The media have worked out
that you have nothing to answer, and we've been through your
files and they show the matter was raised in Parliament in 1991
when Lynda Chalker was Overseas Development Minister and
she gave a robust reply. She also wrote you a long letter on the

subject at the time.' He slides both the letter and the Parliamentary reply across the table.

'Was Ms Nicholson an MP then?' I ask.

'She most certainly was,' says Tony, 'and more importantly, a full investigation was carried out by the Foreign Office, so we're sending all the relevant papers to the police and pointing out that a second inquiry would be an irresponsible waste of public money.'

'So can I sue her for libel?' I ask.

'Not yet,' he replies. 'I talked to the police yesterday, and although they will not release a copy of the letter she sent to them, they made it clear that the accusations were such that they had no choice but to follow them up.'

'If we issue a writ, will she have to release that letter?'

'Yes. It would automatically become part of the evidence.'

'Then we must have grounds to sue her.'

'Not yet,' Tony repeats. 'Let's wait for the police to drop their inquiry before we take any further action. And that could be quite soon, as Radio 4's *Today Programme* have been in touch with Mary. Their research team are also convinced that you have no case to answer, and they want her to appear on the programme.'

'Of course they do,' I say, 'because all they'll want to talk to her about is my appeal.'

'As long as she doesn't discuss the case while an appeal is pending, I'm in favour of her doing the interview.'

'She could of course quote from Lynda Chalker's letter and the Parliamentary reply,' I suggest.

'Why not?' says Tony. 'But let's proceed slowly, step by step.'

'Not something I'm good at,' I admit. 'I prefer proceeding quickly, leap by leap.'

Tony then removes some papers from his briefcase, and tells

me that the appeal will be officially lodged tomorrow. I have to sign an agreement to appeal against sentence, and another against conviction.

Tony would give me a fifty–fifty chance of having the verdict overturned if it were not for the 'Archer' factor. 'If you weren't involved it would be thrown out without a second thought. There wouldn't even have been a trial in the first place.' He puts the odds even higher on getting the sentence reduced. Mr Justice Potts's comment that mine was the worst example of perjury he had ever known has been greeted by the legal profession with raised eyebrows.*

We then turn to the subject of the prison diary, of which I have now completed fifty thousand words, and I warn him that it's going to come as a shock to most of my regular readers. He asks how I'm getting the script through to Alison, remembering this is the tightest-security prison in Europe. I remind him that I am still receiving two to three hundred letters a day, and the censors allow me to turn them round and send them back to my office the following morning, so another ten handwritten pages aren't causing the censor any concern.

'Which reminds me,' I continue, 'could you ask James to wear a cheap watch the next time he visits me, and then I can exchange my Longines.' I hadn't for a moment imagined I would end up in prison, so I was wearing my favourite watch on the day of the verdict, and after twenty years I'd be sorry if it was stolen. James has hankered after it for some time and has already asked me to leave it to him in my will (mercenary brat). 'Will can have the rest of the estate as long as I can have the watch,' James insists. Longines have stopped making that particular slim

---

* Since the court case, Dr Susan Edwards, Associate Dean of Buckingham Law School, has researched every perjury case during the last ten years.

model. Nevertheless, William had agreed to the deal as he considers the overall arrangement very satisfactory.

'I think you'd better wait until you've left Belmarsh before you start swapping watches,' advises Tony. 'And then only when you can be sure that the regulations are a little more relaxed.'

We complete all legal matters, and as he can't escape until the hour is up, we turn our thoughts to the World Athletics Championships in Edmonton, where I had hoped to be spending my summer holiday with Michael Beloff.* Tony tells me the fantastic news that Jonathan Edwards has taken the gold in the triple jump.

'He won easily,' Tony adds, 'clearing nearly eighteen metres. He's so relaxed since his gold in Sydney that I doubt if he will be beaten before the next Olympics at Athens in 2004, and even Mr Justice Potts won't be able to stop you being there to witness that.'

When the prison officer returns to open the door on Tony's side of the room, I leave him in no doubt that the number one priority is sorting out the Kurdish debacle, so that my D-cat can be reinstated as quickly as possible. I also add that I do not require any lawyers to travel to Norfolk at vast expense. They can relay messages through Mary, who's as bright as any of them. Tony smiles, agrees and shakes hands. He has the hands of a heavyweight boxer, and I suspect he'd survive well in prison. They release him, but as I don't have a yellow band around my wrist, I slump back into the seat on the other side of the table and wait.

---

* Michael Beloff QC is an Olympic judge and is allowed to take a guest to the World Championships. His wife Judith has never shown much interest in watching half-naked men running around a track, so we've been a regular 'item' at such events for the past thirty years.

On the circuit we're known as Jack Lemmon and Walter Matthau.

DAY 20

12 noon

In the lunch queue – always a great place to catch up on the gossip – Fletch briefs me on Joseph's problem. I now understand why he couldn't pot a ball on the pool table this morning. When I reach the hotplate, Tony recommends the 'spaghetti vegetarian', which is disguised to look like bolognaise.

'Au gratin?' I suggest.

'Of course, my Lord. Liam, fetch his lordship the grated Parmesan.' A small plastic packet of grated cheese is produced from under the hotplate, opened in front of the duty officer and sprinkled over my spaghetti. This is greeted with a huge round of applause from the prisoners and laughter from the officers. In a lifer's day, this is an event.

Back in my cell I enjoy the dish, but then it is my twentieth day on prison rations. I've been able to take another notch in on my belt. So I reckon I've lost about half a stone.

2.00 pm

When the cell door is opened again, I dash down to the middle level, already dressed in my gym kit, and keep running on the spot by the barred gate. This time I am ticked off the select list of eight from our spur. After a search followed by a route march to another part of the building I've never been to before we arrive in a changing room where we are all supplied with a light blue singlet and dark blue shorts. This, I assume, is just in case any prisoner has spent time at both Oxford and Cambridge.

The gym is divided into two sections. The larger room is the size of a basketball court, where twelve of the prisoners play six-a-side football. We currently have one former Arsenal and Brentford player residing at Belmarsh. There is also a weight-lifting room, about a third of the size of the basketball court, where forty-seven sweaty, tattooed, rippling muscled youths pump iron, so that when they get out of here they will be even more capable of causing grievous bodily harm.

The room is so packed that you can't move more than a few feet without bumping into someone. There are two running machines, two rowing machines and two step machines, in which the younger prisoners show scant interest. I do a six-minute warm-up on the running machine at five miles an hour, which affords me an excellent view of what's going on in the centre of the room. The forty-seven fit young men are pumping weights, not a pretty sight, especially as most of them are simply on an ego trip to establish their status among the other prisoners on the block. I wonder how many of them have worked out that Fletch, Tony, Billy and Del Boy carry the most influence on our spur, and not one of them would be able to locate the gym.

Once I've completed 2,000 metres on the rower in nine minutes, I move on to some light weight-training, before doing another ten minutes on the running machine at eight miles an hour. While I'm running, I begin to notice that many of the lifers have a poor posture. Their backs are not straight, and they swing their shoulders when lifting heavy weights rather than use their arm muscles properly. The two officers in charge can't do much more than keep an eye on what's going on in both rooms. It would be far more sensible to have three sessions of gym each day, with fewer bodies present, then the coach would be able to fulfil a more worthwhile role than just acting as a babysitter. I put this suggestion to one of the officers, and once again they fall back on 'staff shortages'.

After ten minutes on the running machine, I return to the weights before ending on the step machine. When the officer bellows out, 'Last five minutes,' I move on to stretching exercises and complete in one hour exactly the same programme as I would have gone through in the basement gym of my London flat. The only difference is that there, there wouldn't be a murderer in sight.

Back in the changing room, I feel I've done well until Dennis (former Arsenal and Brentford player) joins me and reports that he's scored six goals. I congratulate him, and ask him if it's true that he's been selected to captain Belmarsh for the annual fixture against Holloway? This brings far more laughter and cheers than it deserves, although half the prisoners immediately volunteer to play in goal.

'No, thank you,' says Dennis. 'I've got enough women problems as it is.'

'But you told me that you'd had a good visit on Sunday when your wife and child came to see you?'

'One of my wives,' corrects Dennis. 'And one of my children.'

'How many others do you have?' I ask.

'Three of both,' he admits.

'But that's bigamy,' I say. 'Or possibly trigamy.'

'Get a life, Jeff, I'm not married to any of them. There are no fathers hanging around with shotguns nowadays. They're all partners, not wives. Like a company chairman, I have several shareholders. Thank God I'm banged up in here at the moment,' he adds, 'because if they called an AGM I wouldn't want to have to explain why they won't be getting a dividend this year.'

It's clear that none of the other prisoners listening to this conversation consider it at all unusual, let alone reprehensible. Heaven knows what Britain will be like in fifty years' time if everyone has three 'wives' but doesn't bother to actually marry any of them.

When I return to my cell, I find my canteen order waiting

for me on the bed. I drink mug after mug of water, followed by two KitKats, before going off to have a shower.

4.00 pm

Association. My first assignment is to return a bottle of water to Del Boy (Highland Spring) before searching out Tony to hand over a Mars Bar, followed by Colin (twelve first-class stamps). Having cleared my debts (bubbles) – no one charges me double bubble – I join the other prisoners seated around the television. They're watching the World Athletics Championships. An officer called Mr Hughes brings me up to date on progress so far. After the first day of the decathlon, Macey is leading by one point, and is preparing for his heat in the 110 metre hurdles, which is the first event of the second day. I tell Mr Hughes that Edmonton was where I had originally planned to spend my summer holiday.

'I see that there are a lot of empty seats in the stands,' says Mr Hughes, 'but I find it hard to believe that they're all now in prison.'

Just as Macey goes to his blocks, I spot Joseph standing in the corner – a man who prefers the centre of the room. I leave the World Athletics Championships for a moment to join him.

'Any news of your son?' I ask.

'No.' He looks surprised that I've found out about his problem. 'I've phoned his mother, who says that he's under arrest and she's trying to get in touch with the British Consul. They've got him banged up in a local jail. What are prisons like in Cyprus?' he asks.

'I've no idea,' I tell him. 'Until they sent me to Belmarsh, I didn't know what they were like in England. Just be thankful it's not Turkey. What's he been charged with?'

'Nothing. They found him asleep in a house where some locals had been smoking cannabis, but they've warned him he could end up with a seven-year sentence.'

'Not if he was asleep, surely,' I suggest. 'How old is he?'

'Eighteen, and what makes it worse, while I'm stuck in here I can't do anything about it. My wife says she'll phone the Governor the moment she hears anything.'

'Good luck,' I say, and return to the athletics.

Mr Hughes tells me I missed Macey. He came second in his heat, in a new personal best. 'You can't ask for more than a PB from any athlete,' says Roger Black, the BBC commentator, and adds, 'Stay with us, because it's going to be an exciting day here in Edmonton.'

'Lock-up,' shouts the officer behind the desk at the other end of the room.

I politely point out to the officer that Roger Black has told us we must stay with him.

'Mr Black is there, and I'm here,' comes back the immediate reply, 'so it's lock-up, Archer.'

6.00 pm

Supper. I am now in possession of two tins of Prince's ham (49p), so I take one down to the hotplate to have it opened. Tony adds two carefully selected potatoes, which makes a veritable feast when accompanied by a mug of blackcurrant juice.

After supper I return to work on my script, when suddenly the door is opened by an officer I have never seen before.

'Good evening,' he says. 'I know you'll be off soon, so I wonder if you'd be kind enough to sign this book for my wife. The bookshop told me that it was your latest.'

'I would be happy to do so,' I tell him, 'but it's not mine. It's been written by Geoffrey Archer. I spell my name with a J. It's a problem we've both had for years.'

He looks a little surprised, and then says, 'I'll take it back and get it changed. See you at the same time tomorrow.'

Once I've finished today's script, I read three letters Alison has handed over to Tony Morton-Hooper. One of them is from Victoria Barnsley, the Chairman of my publisher, HarperCollins, saying that she is looking forward to reading *In the Lap of the Gods*, and goes on to let me know that Adrian Bourne, who has taken care of me since Eddie Bell, the former Chairman, left the company, will be taking early retirement. I'll miss them both as they have played such an important role in my publishing career.

The second letter is from my young researcher, Johann Hari, to tell me that he's nearly ready to go over his notes for *In the Lap of the Gods*.* Though he points out that he still prefers the original title *Serendipity*.

The last letter is from Stephan Shakespeare, who was my chief of staff when I stood as Conservative candidate for Mayor of London. His loyalty since the day I resigned brings to mind that wonderful poem by Kipling, 'The Thousandth Man'. Among the many views Stephan expresses with confidence is that Iain Duncan Smith will win the election for Leader of the Conservative Party by a mile.

We won't have to wait much longer to find out if he's right.

---

* The novel has since been renamed *Sons of Fortune*, and I have since changed my publisher to Macmillan.

DAY 21   WEDNESDAY 8 AUGUST 2001

6.03 am

This will be my last full day at Belmarsh. I mustn't make it too obvious, otherwise the press will be waiting outside the gate, and then accompany us all the way to Norfolk. I sit down at my desk and write for two hours.

8.07 am

Breakfast. Shreddies, UHT milk, and an apple. I empty the box of Shreddies, just enough for two helpings.

9.00 am

I am standing in my gym kit, ready for my final session, when Ms Williamson unlocks my cell door and asks if I'm prepared to do another creative-writing class.

'When do you have it planned for?' I ask, not wanting her to know that this is my last day, and I've somehow managed to get myself on the gym rota.

She looks at her watch. 'In about half an hour,' she replies.

I curse under my breath, change out of my gym kit into

slacks and a rather becoming Tiger T-shirt which Will packed for me the day I was sentenced. On my way to the classroom, I pass Joseph at the pool table. He's potting everything in sight, and looking rather pleased with himself.

'Any more news about Justin?' I enquire.

He smiles. 'They've deported him.' He glances at his watch. 'He should be landing at Heathrow in about an hour.' He pots a red. 'His mother will be there to meet him, and I've told her to give him a good clip round the ear.' He sinks a yellow. 'She won't, of course,' he adds with a grin.

'That's good news,' I tell him, and continue my unescorted journey to the classroom.

When I arrive I find Mr Anders, the visiting teacher, waiting for me. He looks a bit put out, so I immediately ask him how he would like to play it.

'Had you anything planned?' he asks.

'Nothing in particular,' I tell him. 'Last week we agreed that the group would bring in something they had written to read to the class, and then we would all discuss it. But not if you had anything else in mind.'

'No, no, that sounds fine.'

This week, nine prisoners and three members of staff turn up. Four of them have remembered to bring along some written work: Colin reads his critique of Frank McCourt's latest book, Tony takes us through his essay on prison reform, which is part of the syllabus for Ruskin College, Oxford, Terry reads a chapter of his novel and we end with Billy's piece on his reaction to hearing that he'd been sentenced to life, and his innermost thoughts during the hours that followed. I choose Billy's work to end on, because as before it was in a different class to any other contribution. I end the session with a few words about the discipline of writing, aware that I would not be with them this time tomorrow. I'm confident that at least three of the group will continue with their projects after I've departed, and that in time Billy's efforts will be published. I will be the first in the queue for a signed copy.

On the way back to my cell, I bump into Liam, who, when he's on the hotplate, always tries to slip me a second ice-cream. He thrusts out his hand and says, 'I just wanted to say goodbye.' I turn red; I've not said a word to anybody following my meeting with Mr Leader, so how has Liam found out?

'Who told you?' I asked.

'The police,' he replied. 'They've agreed to bail, so I'm being released this morning. My solicitor says that probably means that they are going to drop all the charges.'

'I'm delighted,' I tell him. 'But how long have you been in jail?'

'Three and a half months.'

Three and a half months Liam has been locked up in Belmarsh waiting to find out that the police are probably going to drop all the charges. I wish him well before he moves on to shake another well-wisher by the hand. What was he charged with? Perverting the course of justice. A taped phone conversation was the main evidence, which the court has now ruled inadmissible.

Once I'm back on the spur, I phone Alison to let her know that ten more days of the diary are on their way. She tells me that the letters are still pouring in, and she'll forward on to Wayland those from close friends. I then warn her I'm running out of writing pads; could she send a dozen on to Wayland along with a couple of boxes of felt-tip pens? Interesting how I use the word dozen without thinking, despite the fact that decimalization has been with us for over thirty years. In another thirty years, will my grandchildren take the euro for granted and wonder what all the fuss was about?

12 noon

Lunch. Egg and beans, my favourite prison food, but this time I only get one egg because there's an officer sitting where Paul is usually placed. However, Tony still manages a few extra beans.

2.00 pm

I begin writing again, only to be interrupted by three officers marching into my cell: Mr Weedon, accompanied by Mr Abbott and Mr Cook, who are ominously wearing rubber gloves. Mr Weedon explains that this is a cell search – known by prisoners as a spin – and for obvious reasons it has to be carried out without any warning.

'What are you searching for?' I ask.

'Guns, knives, razor blades, drugs, and anything that is against prison regulations. I am the supervising officer,' says Mr Weedon, 'because Mr Cook and Mr Abbott are being tested for the National Vocational Qualification, and this search is part of that test. We will start with a strip-search,' he says, keeping a straight face.

I stand in the middle of my tiny cell, and remove my Tiger T shirt. I then hold my hands high in the air before being asked to turn a complete circle. Mr Abbott then tells me to rub my hands vigorously through my hair, which I do – hidden drugs, just in case you haven't worked it out. This completed, I am allowed to put my T-shirt back on. Mr Cook then asks me to take off my shoes, socks, trousers and pants, all of which are carefully examined by the two junior officers wearing rubber gloves. Once again I am asked to turn a full circle before they invite me to lift the soles of my feet so they can check if I'm wearing any plasters that might be concealing drugs. There are no plasters, so they tell me to get dressed.

'I will now accompany you to a waiting room while your cell is being searched,' Mr Weedon says. 'But first I must ask if you are in possession of anything that belongs to another prisoner, such as guns, knives or drugs?'

'Yes, I have an essay written by Tony Croft, and a poem by Billy Little.' I rummage around in a drawer, and hand them over. They look quickly through them before passing them back. 'I am also in possession of a library book,' I say, trying not to smirk. They try hard not to rise, but they still turn the pages and shake the book about. (Drugs or money this time.)

'I see it's due back today, Archer, so make sure you return it by lock-up, because we wouldn't want you to be fined, would we.' Mr Weedon scores a point.

'How kind of you to forewarn me,' I say.

'Before we can begin a thorough search of your cell,' continues Mr Abbott, 'I have to ask, are you in possession of any legal papers that you do not wish us to read?'

'No,' I reply.

'Thank you,' says Mr Weedon. 'That completes this part of the exercise. Your cell will now be searched by two other officers.'

I was told later that this is done simply for their self-protection, so that should they come across anything illegal, with four officers involved, two sets of two, it becomes a lot more difficult for a prisoner to claim 'it's a set-up, guv' and that whatever was found had been planted.

'Burglars!' I hear shouted by someone at the top of their voice, sounding as if it had come from a nearby cell. I look a little surprised that the officers don't all disappear at speed.

Mr Weedon smiles. 'That's us,' he says. 'We've been spotted, and it's just another prisoner warning his mates that we're out on one of our searching expeditions, so they'll have enough time to dispose of anything incriminating. You'll hear several toilets being flushed during the next few minutes and see a few packages being thrown out of the window.'

Mr Abbott and Mr Cook leave me to be replaced by Ms Taylor and Ms Lynn, who begin to search my cell.

Mr Weedon escorts me to the waiting room on the other side of the spur and locks me in. Bored, I stroll over to the window on the far side of the room, and look down on a well-kept garden. A dozen or so prisoners are planting, cutting, and weeding for a pound an hour. The inmates are all wearing yellow Day-Glo jackets, while the one supervisor is dressed casually in blue jeans and an open-necked shirt. It's a neat, well-kept garden, but then so would anyone's be, if they had a dozen gardeners at a pound an hour.

I am amused to see that one of the prisoners is clipping a hedge with a large pair of shears, quite the most lethal weapon I've seen since arriving at Belmarsh. I do hope they search his cell regularly.

Twenty minutes later I'm let out, and escorted back to Cell 30. All my clothes are in neat piles, my waste-paper bin emptied, and I have never seen my cell looking so tidy. However, the officers have removed my second pillow and the lavatory bleach that Del Boy had so thoughtfully supplied on my first day on Block One.*

6.00 pm

Supper. I take down my second tin of ham (49p) to be opened by a helper on the hotplate. Tony adds two potatoes and a

---

* Bleaching powder can be added to pure heroin, diluting its strength, thus ensuring a larger profit for the dealer. It's against regulations to have two pillows.

spoonful of peas, not all of them stuck together. After I've eaten dinner, I wash my plastic dishes before returning downstairs to join my fellow inmates for Association. I decide to tell only Fletch, Tony and Billy that I'll be leaving in the morning. Fletch said that he was aware of my imminent departure, but didn't realize it was that imminent.

Sitting in his cell along with the others feels not unlike the last day of term at school, when, having packed your trunk, you hang around in the dorm, wondering how many of your contemporaries you will keep in touch with.

Fletch tells us that he's just spent an hour with Ms Roberts, and has decided to appeal against both his sentence and verdict. I am delighted, but can't help wondering if it will affect his decision to allow the contents of the little green book to be published.

'On the contrary,' he says. 'I want the whole world to know who these evil people are and what they've done.'

'But what if they ask you to name the judges, the schoolmasters, the policemen and the politician?'

'Then I shall name them,' he says.

'And what about the other nine children who were put through the same trauma? How do you expect them to react?' Tony asks. 'After all, they must now all be in their late thirties.'

Fletch pulls out a file from his shelf and removes a sheet of paper with the names typed in a single column. 'During the next few weeks I intend to write to everyone named on this list and ask if they are willing to be interviewed by my solicitor. A couple are married and may not even have told their wives or family, one or two will not be that easy to track down, but I'm confident that several of them will back me up, and want the truth to be known.'

'What about ***, **** and *****?'

'I shall name them in court,' Fletch says firmly. '**** of course is dead, but **** and ***** are very much alive.'

Tony starts to applaud while Billy, not given to showing much outward sign of emotion, nods vigorously.

'Lock-up,' hollers someone from the front desk. I shake hands with three men who I had no idea I would meet a month ago, and wonder if I will ever see again.* I return to my cell.

When I reach the top floor, I find Mr Weedon standing by my door.

'When you get out of here,' he says, 'be sure you write it as it is. Tell them about the problems both sides are facing, the inmates and the officers, and don't pull your punches.' I'm surprised by the passion in his voice. 'But let me tell you something you can't have picked up in the three weeks you've spent with us. The turnover of prison staff is now the service's biggest problem, and it's not just because of property prices in London. Last week I lost a first-class officer who left to take up a job as a tube driver. Same pay but far less hassle, was the reason he gave. Good luck, sir,' he says, and locks me in.

9.00 pm

I begin to prepare for my imminent departure. Fletch has already warned me that there will be no official warning, just a knock on my cell door around six-thirty and a 'You're on the move, Archer, so have your things ready.' 'There's only one thing I can guarantee,' he adds. 'Once you've been down to the reception area you will be kept hanging around for at least another hour while an officer completes the paperwork.'

---

*I have already decided, once I'm released I will visit Billy (14 more years) and Fletch (19 more years) if they will allow me to.

DAY 21

9.30 pm

I read through the latest pile of letters, including ones from Mary, Will, and another from Geordie Greig, the editor of *Tatler*, who ends with the words, *There's a table booked for lunch at Le Caprice just as soon as you're out.* No fair-weather friend he.

I then check over the day's script and decide on an early night.

10.14 pm

I turn out the light on Belmarsh for the last time.

DAY 22   THURSDAY 9 AUGUST 2001

4.40 am

I wake from a restless sleep, aware that I could be called at any time. I decide to get up and write for a couple of hours.

6.43 am

I check my watch. It's six forty-three, and there's still no sign of life out there in the silent dark corridors, so I make myself some breakfast. Sugar Puffs, the last selection in my Variety pack, long-life milk and an orange.

6.51 am

I shave, wash and get dressed. After some pacing around my five-by-three cell, I begin to pack. When I say pack, I must qualify that, because you are not allowed a suitcase or a holdall; everything has to be deposited into one of HM Prisons' plastic bags.

7.14 am

I've finished packing but there is still no sign of anyone stirring. Has my transfer been postponed, cancelled even? Am I to remain

DAY 22

at Belmarsh for the rest of my life? I count every minute as I pace up and down, waiting to make my official escape. What must it be like waiting to be hanged?

7.40 am

I empty the last drop of my UHT milk into a plastic mug, eat a McVitie's biscuit, and begin to wonder if there is anyone out there. I reread Mary's and Will's letters. They cheer me up.

8.15 am

My cell door is at last opened by a Mr Knowles.

'Good morning,' he says cheerfully. 'We'll be moving you just as soon as we've got all the remand prisoners off to the Bailey.' He checks his watch. 'So I'll be back around 9.30. If you'd like to take a shower, or if there's anything else you need to do, I'll leave your door open.'

Forgive the cliché, but I breathe a sigh of relief to have it confirmed that I really am leaving. I take a shower – I've now mastered the palm, press, soap, palm, press method.

During the next hour several prisoners drop by to say farewell as the news spreads around the spur that I'm departing. Del Boy relieves me of my last bottle of water, saying he could get used to it. Once he's left, I suggest to an officer that I would like to give my radio to one of the prisoners who never gets a visit. The officer tells me that it's against the regulations.

'To give something to someone in need is against the regulations?' I query.

'Yes,' he replies. 'You may be trying to bribe him, or repay him for a supply of drugs. If you were seen giving a radio to another prisoner, you would immediately be put on report and your sentence might even be lengthened by twenty-eight days.'

My problem is that I just don't think like a criminal.

I wait until the officer is out of sight, then nip downstairs and leave the radio and a few other goodies on Fletch's bed. He'll know whose needs are the greatest.

9.36 am

Mr Knowles returns to escort me to the reception area where I first appeared just three long weeks ago. I am placed in a cubicle and strip-searched, just as I was on the day I arrived. Once I've put my clothes back on, they handcuff me – only for the second time – and then lead me out of the building and into what I would describe as a Transit van. Down the left-hand side are four single seats, one behind each other. On the right-hand side is a cubicle in which the prisoner is placed like some untamed lion. Once I'm locked in, I stare out of the little window for some time, until, without any warning, the vast electric barred gates slide slowly open.

As the black Transit van trundles out of Belmarsh, I have mixed feelings. Although I am delighted and relieved to be leaving, I'm also anxious and nervous about being cast into another world, having to start anew and form fresh relationships all over again.

It has taken me three weeks to pass through Hell. Am I about to arrive in Purgatory?

extracts reading groups
competitions books new
books discounts extracts extracts
competitions extracts discounts events
books new reading groups
reading groups new extracts discounts reading groups
events books
new books extracts
new titles reading groups
interviews
reading groups events extracts extracts books
books discounts new interviews
new books events events extracts
events new interviews books
discounts extracts discounts
www.panmacmillan.com
extracts events reading groups books
competitions books extracts new

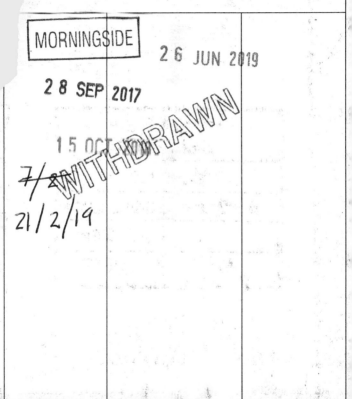